Find Grant Funding Now!

Find Grant Funding Now!

The Five-Step Prosperity Process for Entrepreneurs and Business

Sarah Beth Aubrey

WILEY

Published by John Wiley & Sons, Inc., Hoboken, New Jersey.

Published simultaneously in Canada.

For general information on our other products and services or for technical support, please contact our Customer Care Department within the United States at (800) 762-2974, outside the United States at (317) 572-3993 or fax (317) 572-4002.

Wiley publishes in a variety of print and electronic formats and by print-on-demand. Some material included with standard print versions of this book may not be included in e-books or in print-on-demand. If this book refers to media such as a CD or DVD that is not included in the version you purchased, you may download this material at http://booksupport.wiley.com. For more information about Wiley products, visit www.wiley.com.

Library of Congress Cataloging-in-Publication Data:
Aubrey, Sarah Beth.
  Find grant funding now! : the five-step prosperity process for entrepreneurs and business / Sarah Beth Aubrey.
    pages cm. — (Wiley nonprofit authority)
  Includes index.
  ISBN 978-1-118-71048-7 (hardback); ISBN 978-1-118-71040-1 (ebk); ISBN 978-1-118-71041-8 (ebk)
  1. New business enterprises—Finance.   2. Small business—Finance.   3. Grants-in-aid.
I. Title.
  HG4027.6.A93 2014
  658.15'224—dc23
                                                                    2013030214

Printed in the United States of America

10 9 8 7 6 5 4 3 2 1

This book is for Cary as we enter the New Era. ILU

Contents

CONTENTS

CONTENTS

PART THREE
Application, Award, Afterward

CONTENTS

Preface

Grants are never free. No matter the source, the kind of funding we'll be talking about in this book is never without a cost. When approaching grant funding always consider the most useful purpose for that money. Here's a mantra to keep in mind: *Grants are a privilege, not a right.*

No matter where the grant money originates, be it from federal sources or a charitable foundation, endeavor to use grants responsibly, with regard to how they might best be invested, and with as much leverage from other sources as possible. Now, let's uncover the truth about the grant industry and grant writing. First, I'll start with a fact:

Most likely, your grant writing efforts will fail.

That seems a harsh way to begin, doesn't it? I won't apologize for the truth, though. Reading basic how-to books about grant writing will not win a grant. Hiring a grant writer to prepare your application will not win a grant. Studying endless examples of perfect grant narratives and poring over evocative statements of need will not guarantee one cent of grant money. If you simply approach grants in the typical how-to way, you'll probably just fail. But, there is a path to success with grants.

Do you visualize your success? Do you put thought into the direction in which your business is going? If so, you're a strategizer, and you'll need that approach to winning grants. Grant success is not just about the application process; it begins long before that. It begins with solid planning and, yes, visualizing time. Grants fail because of a lack of strategic intent and no clear direction. Application forms, narrative writing, and gathering documentation are all just going through the motions of grant writing, but without real planning they don't alone yield cash.

This is a strategic book, not a how-to book. It's strategy-heavy and tactics-light. Today, the consulting industry works to sell outcomes, not services and deliverables. My practice in the area of finding funding works the same way. Grant seekers are not interested in the tactics involved to assemble reams of paper. They are seeking *money*. There are other relevant outcomes besides money from using grants, and I'll share those, too, because I think you'll appreciate considering additional benefits. Ultimately, though, grants should be used as part of a financial plan. With that in mind, I focus on providing you the pieces of the big picture that I believe most grant writing books and course overlook.

IT'S THE STRATEGY, NOT THE HOW-TO

In his recent book, *The Charge: Activating the 10 Human Drives That Make You Feel Alive*, author and productivity consultant Brendon Burchard talks about motivation. He says that in this abundant world where many of our needs are fulfilled we subsequently spend much time, energy, and money seeking our wants. Burchard also comments that we tend to be less happy now than we've been in recent decades. One of his arguments is that people lack a strategy that works to seek and find that happiness and success they so desperately want. He writes:

> [A]ny lack of charge you feel in your life is only the result of a colossal failure in strategy. Only the failure to strategically control the contents of your consciousness keeps you from feeling the consistent internal charge of being fully alive, engaged, connected, and fulfilled.[1]

This book is a *strategy* book. Because of that, you might consider it required reading in advance of all the other titles you may subsequently read that tell you exactly how to write a grant, but nothing about why and when to use grants. You already know that to get what you want you must be better than the competition. This applies to grants as well; you must "get it" way more than the other people seeking cash from the same well.

---

1. Brendan Burchard, *The Charge: Activating the 10 Human Drives That Make You Feel Alive* (London: Simon & Schuster, 2012), iii.

Find Grant Funding Now! draws on my personal experience and is designed to serve other entrepreneurs. I'm offering you a real grant writer's guide, not an academic's soliloquy of hypothetical theories. This book goes beyond simple tips to craft flawless narratives and bulletproof budgets to show you why some proposals get funded and others do not.

I find money for entrepreneurs, small-business people, and communities. Primarily, I endeavor to secure grants, a large portion of them federal, though grants from individual states and private foundations also enter my radar screen. While I do have a handful of "grant certifications" and have taken some courses, I am self-taught. My academic degree is in communications, and I spent my early career freelance-writing for trade journals as well as working on market research and feasibility study reports. That training lent itself nicely to grant preparation since clear presentation of ideas is paramount to successful grant proposals. However, you'll see that winning grants has very little to do with exceptional writing skills and more to do with project management and especially the choices you make before applying—the most important choice of all is whether to apply or pass the opportunity by. Good news: You are already inclined to understand the value in creating a niche and replicating that tactic or product, filling a market need, and finding a way to come up with a better strategy. You understand that going through the motions is a mediocre life and a mediocre business strategy. These traits will serve you well if you choose to consider using grants for business, personal projects, and community projects that you support. But, the grant funding world is different and confusing for the uninitiated. Even if you hire someone to help, that may not offer you the pre-work you need to understand how grant funding takes a unique approach. Frankly, you've got to do better than just hiring a $40/hour consultant from an association's website listing. You, not the contractor, should develop a basic understanding about the industry that will enable you to assemble the right team to build the application after you've determined only the best grant programs to tackle. I want you to go after only your most-likely-to-win grants, leaving the rest to shotgun-approach people who apparently would rather work a lot than work smart.

My point in sharing what I know in this book is that I am an entrepreneur, too. I enjoy seeing an unfilled market niche and going after it. I love the thrill of a new opportunity and supporting sound projects that need money to implement. I know that regular individuals and businesses can use grants. You can teach yourself how to write and prepare them or you can hire a grant professional; either way, you're much better off knowing some really good tips and you'll gain them here. So, to help you work smart, take a look at the following features.

THIS BOOK'S ORGANIZATION

As an entrepreneur, I always direct my business destiny. Even though I contract experts in areas where I need support, I never simply turn everything over and walk away. If I have a need, there's a reason and I stay engaged to ensure my need is properly met. As a grant funding consultant, prospects sometimes contact my office in the hopes of employing someone to do the opposite—they want to believe that since they hired a grant writer, the next correspondence we'll have is when they receive a check. It's just not true. Winning grants is a strategic effort. If you hired a firm to come in and do a strategic planning session for your company, you would expect to be involved. The same goes for grant funding. You, the applicant, must take an active role. If you approach grant funding as a strategic initiative, and not simply "someone else's job" to get you the money, your chances for success are strong.

If you don't hire a grant professional, you need the strategy and the how-to. This book accomplishes both. I advocate getting grant educated to get grant funded. However, if you don't plan to make grant preparing your career, you don't have time or interest in lengthy descriptions of how to write the perfect narrative. That is not contained within these pages; *Find Grant Funding Now!* is a grab-and-go kind of guide—it's ready to use. Navigating the grant funding marketplace is a big adventure, but I've broken it out into manageable sections. Here are some resources that keep the book's tempo quick and the content you need convenient.

My grant consulting practice is built around the premise of employing a process that has been honed over time by the grit of failures and buffed and polished by the shine of successes. I've built the *Five-Step Prosperity Process* that we'll call upon in every chapter.

Five-Step Prosperity Process:
1. Project
2. Peruse
3. Ponder
4. Prepare
5. Patience

Each step directs the flow of conversation. The book is organized by chapters, but uses this process in each chapter. Here's a general breakdown of the flow of the book:

Part One covers Chapters 1 through 4 and centers around the topic of navigating the federal agency funding process. Chapter 1explores the *why*, that is, why grants and why now. We'll look at the size of the grant funding marketplace and give you the idea of what is out there for the asking. In Chapter 2, I delve into my process and cover each of the action steps in detail. Refer back to this chapter if you need help connecting the steps to your actions and why. If you want to really understand the meaning of the word *grant*, read Chapter 3. This section dissects my definition of the word and presents examples of other financial vehicles that seem like grants but are not. In Chapter 4, we look at the funders. This chapter is a solid discussion of what's out there and who's got the money—read and reread!

In Part Two, Chapters 5 through 8 are all about the strategic aspects of grant funding. In Chapter 5, I explain how to find the money and search for it efficiently. We cover a lot of ground here, including how to determine feasibility and eligibility as well as how to read a grant announcement. In Chapter 6, I work through things you can fund with grants and projects you typically cannot. Chapter 7 gets into the implications of accepting grant funds and strategic considerations all applicants should bear in mind before they sign the grant agreement. Assembling a solid project team wins grant applications when you have a great group. I cover this component, including my top tips for selecting a project manager, in Chapter 8.

Finally, Part Three is about the packaging and waiting game. I reserved this section for last because much of this base material can be found in other works. This is my unique take on these topics, but "How to write a grant" is an oft-written-about topic. Still, you've come this far; grab some ideas from me that fit the rest of the system from Chapters 9 through 12. In Chapter 9, we work through the components of most grant applications. In Chapter 10, I teach you how to score your application, even if the grant agency doesn't provide a score sheet. Chapter 11 is all about survival—surviving the wait for an answer—and Chapter 12 is a final word on my top tips for the best application you can make; flip to it right now and get ten grant writing secrets you can implement today!

In addition to the five-step process, I've included other tools for developing your grant strategy. Two assessments appear in the appendix:

1. Take the Project Evaluation first; you may want to take this very early in the reading of this book and again as you gain more knowledge.

2. The Grant Planning Tool is a document I use with my own prospects and clients to help them determine where they are in the readiness to pursue funding successfully.

Both of these are available for download at our special website for readers, www.findgrantfundingnow.com. This site also includes links to the full Prosperity Consulting website where readers can gain access to many more free tools and other companion products, including:

- A signup page to receive e-mail updates with grant writing tips

- Methods to participate in the exclusive grant questions forum for networking with other entrepreneurs and get answers straight from the author

- Access to special program and course discounts

The website complements this text and will change regularly to keep readers up-to-date on the latest additions for tips and grant ideas. The forum allows networking between entrepreneurs looking for many of the same answers and helps develop relationships that can lead to successful project implementation.

Consulting practices are characterized by a series of regular conversations around the consultant's topic of expertise. Like most executives, I discuss similar challenges and opportunities with the bulk of my clientele. Rather than looking at that as mundane, the entrepreneur in me sees an opportunity in the patterns that naturally emerge. Indeed, one reason I wrote this book is to share my ideas on these oft-repeated questions with a broad audience. So, I've organized each chapter by conversations, many of them taken exactly from the fabric of my day job. During those conversations, at the top of each chapter, I pose questions I often hear and throughout the chapter I provide my answers. It's like a one-on-one grant strategy session you can refer back to anytime.

SPECIAL ELEMENTS

Entrepreneurs use tools and like implementation. I understand that. So, I created this book to be informative but also practical. Besides the assessments I mentioned in the previous section, you'll find the following peppered throughout the book to help strengthen your ability to take the concepts you read here and apply them immediately.

- **Grants Guru Glossary:** My topic can be a tad technical. Rather than hiding the glossary at the end (who has time to flip to the glossary while reading?), I pull the word or phrase from the text and define it right there. This feature is called the Grants Guru Glossary, so pay attention; it's a word or phrase you need to know.

- **Jump Ahead:** I am a skimmer. I'm easily bored; I especially like to see what's up ahead. Knowing fellow entrepreneurs often have the same tendencies, I have provided something

I call *jump-aheads* in each chapter. I employ these features when I'm covering an issue that naturally leads to questions about a related topic. The jump-aheads will direct you to the chapter where more on a particular topic can be read. I don't want you to feel tied to reading everything *A* to *Z* in order to benefit. I've ordered the book to follow the course I believe works best—but you're an entrepreneur! You know your business; review the topics in the order I present them or jump ahead as desired.

- **Perspectives on Prosperity:** You'll find this section, *Perspectives on Prosperity*, at the conclusion of each chapter. Given that the word *prosperity* is part of my business name, I collect prosperity statements and phrases and enjoy analyzing them. These quotes are about the process of learning. Entrepreneurship is anybody's game right now. It's not just for the young and ambitious or the mature and experienced. It's about life choices. Savvy entrepreneurs are lifelong learners who know that investigating something new, or even something old with a new spin, is worth doing if it means an opportunity for the business.

- **Website:** Visit www.findgrantfundingnow.com to download the grant planning and evaluation tools found in this book's appendix, as well as to sign up to receive e-mail updates with grant writing tips and comment in the forum. Buyers of this book who visit the site can also find special program access and course discounts.

This book will help you make sound judgments about grant funding. The decision to *not* spend time and money applying is worth a fortune, so read on to gain insights about when and where grants are effectively used, hot areas for funding right now, and how to determine when grants really don't fit at all.

Acknowledgments

Books are creations requiring multiple layers of involvement including important collaborators beyond the author alone. Most readers would assume this, and all authors certainly know it. Friends, family, employees, and other significant people in an author's tightly knit community live that involvement with the author during the process—they share the enthusiasm, the frustration, the time commitment, the missed commitments, the over-commitments, and in general, the positives and negatives of taking a book from concept to shelf. In light of this, I certainly have my share of those to thank.

In the summer of 2012, I the made decision to write a book about my experiences as a grant consultant. I felt the need to help entrepreneurs understand what was involved in achieving grant funding and I wanted to let them know what I saw as an industry largely unexplored by small-business owners. Initially, I planned to package an e-book or maybe build out a larger nonfiction work and self-publish. I had gone so far as to contact a few digital printers and was close to signing with one when I attended the NSA (National Speaker's Association) National Convention in July. On a last-minute whim I ventured into a benefit seminar prior to the general conference opening. The focus of this event was around different publishing options for speakers/consultants. Considering that timely, I settled in. One of the panelists was literary agent Jeff Herman, owner of the Jeff Herman Agency. I was acquainted with Jeff's work, though he didn't know me. Way back in 2005, I had purchased his signature book, *Jeff Herman's Guide to Book Publishers, Editors, and Literary Agents*, and used it to educate myself about the publishing world. Upon reading it then, I decided that in fact I didn't need an agent and I went on to sell my first two titles, one to Storey Publishing and one to Howell Bookhouse, on my own. Those books continue to sell, but I knew I was ready for more with the message

I had to offer with the "grant business book" I'd been plotting. So, I met Jeff and left with encouragement after he requested a proposal on my book. Ultimately, I signed Jeff as my agent and he wowed me with the volume of inquiries I received following his shopping around of my proposal and the speed with which we found the right publisher. He deserves my thanks for the opportunity to work with Wiley on what is now *Find Grant Funding Now!: The Five-Step Prosperity Process for Entrepreneurs and Business*.

I also wish to offer thanks to the NSA. What a powerhouse organization! I'm so fortunate to be a member and to become acquainted with the amazing professionals I meet at every event. Keep up the good work—especially the networking opportunities that abound from your conferences. Had it not been for NSA, I wouldn't have met Jeff Herman. Interestingly, following the National Convention where my book went from idea to pitch, at my very next NSA live event I was signing my agreement to work with Wiley, which was fortuitous.

Speaking of Wiley, I'd like to thank my acquisitions editor, Susan McDermott, and my original content development editor, Jennifer MacDonald, also deserves a world of thanks. She's been so helpful teaching me a few new tricks about preparing the manuscript and making me a better author with her suggestions to tighten the content and smooth the flow of my ideas to the page—great work!

My office staff is small, consisting primarily of contractors and short-term professionals who work project-by-project. Still, I have my "regulars." Oh, *thank you* to these stalwart friends! It is very difficult to take time off from your client commitments to write a book, as my team can now attest. Thank you so very much to Erin Smith Robinson for her gracious acceptance of my wayward ways during this writing period.

As is my tradition, I also like to give a shout-out to a member of my immediate family. The acknowledgments section is as good a place as any. So, Tom Potter, this time the nod goes to you! Tom is my youngest sibling and the only fellow entrepreneur among the five of us kids. Tom, I wish you all the best in your business-building pursuits and much happiness in life as you enjoy the satisfaction of working for yourself. I'm proud of you.

ACKNOWLEDGMENTS

The final thank-you for this work goes to my husband, Cary Aubrey. While I would thank him anyway for putting up with my general absence the last three months as I've worked through this book, he deserves a very unique acknowledgment for this book in particular. I owe this book entirely to C. A. He convinced me to start the grant writing business. He is also my biggest proponent and motivator when I've been afraid of failure.

In a performance-based business, it's win or lose, so the pressure to please is a daily fact of life. Sometimes it gets the best of me, and when that happens, Cary makes sure I brush it off and get back to work. He is also very supportive of my work, though it's been at a cost to his free time. More times than I can count, he has made me dinner and carried it to my office when I'm working late. He's filled my car with gas when I'm running late and he's never complained when I've made us a day late for a trip we were planning because I had a grant submission deadline. Cary has made more photocopies, stuffed more envelopes, and made more 8 P.M. FedEx drop-offs than anyone I know, including me. All these things have been done on Sundays or late at night, and, of course, he doesn't get paid. Cary, you are the best and your patience is exceptional. A person once told me that if you want to fly, you need a ground crew. Cary, thank you for being my crew chief. I love you!

About the Author

 **Sarah Aubrey** is a thought leader in the world of grant funding strategy and acquisition, particularly for entrepreneurs. Raised on a farm in East Central Illinois, she has been developing freelance businesses since she could write. From her home office in an old, two-story farmhouse she has won over 500 grants in 38 states and Puerto Rico; funding has yielded $55 million. Recently named to the *Indianapolis Business Journal*'s "Forty Under 40," this National Speakers Association member brings a serial entrepreneur's take on keynoting with a country girl's practical, encouraging messaging style. As the owner of Prosperity Consulting, LLC, a Certified Women's Business Enterprise, she hosts grant training courses four times each year, speaks at industry events, and and consults with businesses and communities about the strategy behind find, winning, and using grant funding.

Her previous two books focused on her experiences in developing niche small-farm and local food initiatives. *Starting and Running Your Own Small Farm Business* was released in January 2008. Her second book, released in late 2009 by Howell Book House, is titled *The Profitable Hobby Farm.*

If you want exact steps for grant writing, visit www.prosperity consultingsba.com and join the free monthly newsletter or gain weekly tips by signing up for the MidWeek Motivation blog.

PART ONE

Navigating the Grant and Funding Landscape

CHAPTER ONE

Why Grants *Now*?

You've never considered using grants and didn't even know they were open to businesses. You've always heard they were a lot of red tape. Why bother with grant funding *now*?

"So, how much grant money is really out there?"

"Is the grant industry even worth my time?"

"What do grant agencies really fund, anyway? I thought every grant went to academics and 'save the *blah, blah, blah*' whatever foundation . . . "

"Do you really think we ought to use grants? Whose money is it, anyway?"

"I'm not sure how to describe what I want to do, but I know I'll need money—is there a grant for that?"

A great many of my initial conversations with anyone I meet begin with the inevitable opener, "So, what do you do?" Actually, I love answering this question. Questions about grant funding are the reason my business exists. The process of working though questions and answers like those above is what got me started consulting about grants (I'll explain more in a few chapters), and now I employ a certain set of questions to help people find money, as you'll see in my self-assessment tools found later in the book. Because grant seeking is a highly subjective business, it's also a very relational business where I need to learn as much as I can about the project and goals. When a new client retains me, the process often goes the same with the questions and answers. I ask a lot of questions before we ever talk about building a grant application.

The longer I worked in the industry, the more questions I had about the reasons behind interest in grant funding. I began to wonder: *Why grants, why now? What makes this topic interesting?* While not a new phenomenon, grant funding as a means of the overall financial strategy is gaining in popularity and acceptance in the private sector. Where it was once believed that the pool of funds was solely reserved for academia and nonprofit work, businesses, small and large, established and emerging, are looking into both creating grant programs to support their causes and using grant money to complete work. What is going on to make an old stand-by—grant writing—suddenly like a new trend? Why grants now?

WHY GRANT FUNDING IS HOT

That's an easy question to begin with, though it's a matter of opinion. Every time I give a speech about grant funding in the private sector, I like to lead with three questions:

1. How many audience members have ever wanted to start their own business or work for themselves as a freelancer?

2. How many have ever considered using some alternative kind of funding besides a bank loan?

3. How many who said yes to number one have ever considered using grant dollars?

The results are always similar in my little qualitative market research poll. Everyone in the room, be it a group of 6 or 600, will say yes to #1. This group includes quite a few people who will later admit that they will never actually become an entrepreneur, just that they love the notion of it. As for #2, about half of the room says yes to considering funding besides the traditional financing industry—and this number is growing rapidly. For #3, rarely do I have audience members tell me they've used or considered grants, even if they wanted other ideas for finding funds.

People of all backgrounds are right now exceptionally curious, hungry, and largely seeking to do more on their own. People today are rather willing to go it alone; many are starting businesses or are thinking about it as a *someday* goal. According to the Ewing Marion Kaufmann Foundation, a foundation that is devoted to entrepreneurship, approximately 540,000 new businesses are created each month of every year, even (*especially*) during the recent recession.[1] What are the reasons for this boom? Economists using labor and wage statistics could mount a case that this movement toward DIY (do-it-yourself) is economic. Some would suggest we've reached our capacity for doing jobs of rote and desire deeply to express our pent-up creativity. No matter—DIY approaches are hugely popular in everything from making your own wedding decorations to funding a business. Investment in the DIY movement, particularly in social media, is strong. Consider the exploding popularity of social sharing site, www.pinterest.com. Its members create pages and share them just as a means to adorn a public place with their personalized *pins*, that is, images of anything that interests them. This site encourages not just crafting, creating, and collecting, but sharing and conversing about how to make or build those items that interest the person who pins it and fellow members who see it or even *re-pin* the item, thereby expressing their interest. At present, all this pinning isn't amounting to exceptional profits—at least not as of this writing. "Pinterest is part of a group of startups that offer twists on Internet networking among various groups. They typically have little discernible profit or revenue, but have landed some outsized investments from venture capitalists," reports Sarah McBride in an article in the February 20, 2013 issue of *Reuters*. The article also reports that the valuation of the market is presently worth $2.5 billion with more dollars flowing toward the Internet startups of the do-it-yourself set, such as Pinterest.[2]

---

1. Ewing Marion Kauffman Foundation, www.kauffman.org.
2. Sarah McBride, *Start Up Pinterest Wins New Funding, $2.5 billion Valuation,* online http://www.reuters.com/article/2013/02/21/net-us-funding-pinterest-idUSBRE91K01R20130221.

If the market isn't yet large, why does it matter? I believe it shows a trend in the way small businesses are emerging. Sure, some new entrepreneurs start a business almost as a last resort when the corporate world fails them—that's the *hungry* part of my earlier comment.

Others are curious to see how easy it might be to begin a company today given that operating online has both a low initial investment and theoretically an instant marketplace. I'm not sure what is in store for the DIY world of business, but it appears that the ability to leap from idea to launch is happening much quicker today.

Like anything too casual, though, are new entrepreneurs serious enough? Are they leaping out just as easily as hopping in? That's a possibility, too. The Small Business Administration (SBA) reports that an estimated 552,600 new employer firms opened for business in 2009, and 660,900 firms closed.[3] Businesses without employees, called *non-employer firms* by SBA and often referred to as *solopreneurs* on the street, are opening and closing much more often. SBA says they turn over nearly three times as often as those companies with a payroll.

It is a positive thing to see small businesses opening, but why are so many closing and, worse yet, filing for bankruptcy? Take a look at SBA's open, close, and bankruptcy chart in Table 1.1 as an illustration of the trend. Items with an 'e' behind them represent best estimates as of the date the data was published.

Startup owners know there is potential to fail or just fade away. Facts reported by the U.S. Department of Commerce, Census Bureau, Business Dynamics Statistics, U.S. Dept. of Labor, and

TABLE 1.1 Starts and Closures of Employer Firms, 2005–2009

Category	2005	2006	2007	2008	2009
Births	644,122	670,058	668,395	626,400e	552,600e
Closures	565,745	599,333	592,410	663,900e	660,900e
Bankruptcies	39,201	19,695	28,322	43,546	60,837

Source: U.S. Small Business Administration (www.sba.gov), April 17, 2013.

---

3. U.S. Small Business Administration, www.sba.gov (April 17, 2013).

Bureau of Labor Statistics seem to endorse the notion of exploring unique financing alternatives. According to the SBA's website: "Seven out of 10 new employer firms survive at least 2 years, half at least 5 years, a third at least 10 years, and a quarter stay in business 15 years or more."[4]

What's happening to entrepreneurs early in the businesses? Do they run out of motivation, or money? If it's money, and it's always about money at some point, here's the quandary: Financing availability from traditional sources can be tough. Not everyone qualifies for a traditional bank loan, and frankly, not everyone wants one. Part of the culture of distrust breeding the growth in general of DIY includes concerns of uncertainty about the financial services industry. Regularly, startup owners come to me for grant funding and yet have no desire to take out a bank loan. Reasons to avoid the lending marketplace are varied, but some I've heard include fears of being tied down to a repayment schedule if the business experiences rough patches, a general feeling of skepticism that their lender will be there for them or remain stable, and even an internal philosophy toward avoidance of debt. Younger people often say their interest in grants comes from the age-old story of not wanting to end up like their parents. I'm not talking about "staying cool" and not becoming fuddy-duddies or wearing black knee-socks with white walking shoes, either.

> Generations X and Y want freedom to self-direct their lives; they don't want to be on the hamster-wheel of debt that they've watched generations before tie themselves to, working in something they hate because they need the money.

Attitudes about employment are shifting, too. Generations X and especially Y resist the 8-to-5 grind and demand flexible schedules far more than any previous generation ever deemed conceivable. Many of them believe entrepreneurship is the answer. But does it work out?

---

4. U.S. Small Business Administration, http://web.sba.gov/faqs/faqindex .cfm?areaID = 24 (April 17, 2013).

The SBA does appear to claim the trend toward business failures is improving and optimism is the new tone. In a recent article entitled "Small Business Trends, Small Business, Big Impact," the agency comments that "while corporate America has been downsizing, the rate of small business startups has grown, and the rate for small business failures has declined."[5]

Whether you view the proverbial glass as half empty or half full, statistically speaking, entrepreneurs only have a 50/50 chance of making it to a five-year anniversary.

Let's say you don't get a loan, but instead find investors—that doesn't guarantee longevity, either. Adding more money at startup does not appear to be the answer for business health, either. Even those companies backed by a source beyond self-funding are unprotected from closure during the early years. The numbers are startling. In September 2012, the *Wall Street Journal* reported that the National Venture Capital Association estimates that between 25 and 30 percent of venture-backed businesses still fail.[6]

> Clearly, all entrepreneurs need creative financing—especially now as a wave of corporate dropouts, early retirees, and unemployed recent college grads surges toward self-directed business.

There are a lot of people launching entrepreneurial endeavors. Creative marketing and technology have long been the hallmark of the American Ideal. Creative funding strategies are emerging, too; grants may be one of those options for you. I have no desire to give you the notion that grants prevent failure any more than any other kind of cash, but with so many people looking at starting their own companies and so much confusion about financing them, you need every tool available. For some readers, grants may provide another option when venture capital (VC) backers walk away or when the traditional financing community is timid about lending to your new

5. http://www.sba.gov/content/small-business-trends.
6. Deborah Gage, *The Venture Capital Secret: 3 Out of 4 Start-Ups Fail*, online. wsj.com/article/SB10000872396390443720204578004980476429190.html.

enterprise. This book offers an idea I believe is underexplored in the business realm.

Ultimately, if you need money, you may have to hunt for it yourself. The business startup world right now looks like a Solar System of planets spinning off their axes and all converging toward some unseen force at the same time: People young and mature are hungry for work, all ages seek motivation and meaning, DIY and a yearning to share something that matters are budding everywhere, distrust in the same-old-thing is rampant, and it's now becoming acceptable to set up a website and ask strangers to fund your business with online gifts.

In an arrangement now referred to as *crowdfunding* investors may never meet their potential entrepreneurs and the closest thing to a business plan they may ever see is a homemade video of the company owner's plea for funding. Small-biz developers also tell me they must leverage their own dollars, and money coming in from other sources, including traditional bank and venture capital financing, as well as small investors ranging from family to online crowdsourcing groups. Massolution, a research firm tracking crowdsourcing, reports that 16.9 percent of the $2.7 billion crowdsourcing industry's activity comes from small business. In an article written by Oliver St. John for *USA Today*, he notes that *crowdfunding*, that is, the solicitation of money in the form of donations or investment online, especially via social media, is growing rapidly. It appears crowdfunding is a legitimate avenue for even the most traditional of industries.[7]

It should be noted that while Crowdfunding and crowdsourcing are often now used interchangeably, it appears that Crowdfunding grew organically out of the notion of crowdsourcing. According to the authors of the book *CrowdFund Investing for Dummies*: "Crowdsourcing is the online gathering of a group of people to share knowledge and wisdom to build a better product." The authors go on to point out that Crowdfunding is really the financial outgrowth of a community, or 'crowd' that has been created and as such

---

7. Oliver St. John, "Crowdfunding to Build a Farm: E-I-E-I-Dough," *USA Today* (23 May 2013).

when funding is requested, investors can support the community's cause through online donations thereby creating the Crowdfunding concept.[8]

Project funding does not have to be entirely self-financed or borrowed, but business developers always tell me they need to leverage both their money and funds from the litany of other sources available now. Enter grants as a potential cost-sharing vehicle. While grants require certain skills, these can be learned and used again and again.

REGULATIONS, RULES, AND RED TAPE

When working with grants, there will be at least one or all of my dreaded five *R*s: rules, requirements, regulations, recordkeeping, and reporting. Truthfully, there are major drawbacks to using grants—the kinds of drawbacks that are particularly unappealing to entrepreneurs. For starters, just the notion of being in business with the government is a negative to many. According to a March 2013 economic trends survey compiled by the National Federation of Independent Business (NFIB), the number-one growth problem small businesses report is taxes, followed by government requirements, and in general the notion of red tape.[9]

"Ugh," you might be thinking. "If there is red tape, let's walk!" That's understandable, but most entrepreneurs are already cavorting with a few of the five *R*s in their businesses. Learning how to work with grant programs is an important first step. Obviously, this is a still a fair question and certainly, like all questions around grant funding, a common question. I get into this conversation with prospects, friends, and clients with all measures of political persuasion and understanding of our government. It's legitimate on any front. Let me give you my thoughts on the matter.

---

8. Jason W. Best, Zak Corion-Cassady, and Sherwood Neiss, *Crowdfund Investing for Dummies*, February 2013, Wiley.
9. National Federation of Independent Business, http://www.nfib.com/Portals/0/PDF/sbet/sbet201304.pdf.

My first response is simple: Not all grants come from governmental sources.

Many grants that fit entrepreneurs, especially for innovation, come from private and corporate foundations. Social-responsibility giving, including giving to foundations that then support the

> Not all grants come from governmental sources. If you have qualms about using tax dollars to support a project, then you still may find a grant that can work and maintain that principal.

causes, new products, services, and industries the giver cares about, is on the rise. Foundation giving makes up almost *2 percent of our GDP*, according to the *Chronicle of Philanthropy*.[10] The Center for Philanthropy at Indiana University goes even further with the statistic saying that contributions to social causes amount to $732 per person per year in America today. Not all of this money is given for charity—as much as 25 percent is used to fund grant programs that support the organization's mission.

JUMP AHEAD

To learn about grant agency types, jump ahead to Chapter 3.

The second part of my response is much more complicated. There are government grants available for businesses and yet there are concerns about the use of these funds for businesses. The profile of this topic has been elevated in the last four years, and it's a fair debate. Regardless of the bad press many failed grant-funded projects have received, I still see a growing interest in applying for and using government grants. This interest is not only from types you might think of as traditional grant seekers, such as academia and researchers. No; calls come into my office from a wide variety of small-business people.

They are seeking project funding for themselves, their communities, and the causes they support. That funding exists, and many

---

10. *The Chronicle of Philanthropy*, Philanthropy.com/section (2012).

fleet, regulation-averse business owners are taking it. Is that a conundrum or just a contradiction?

I think it's both and I think it's human nature. I know it's the nature of entrepreneurs who live to come up with their own way, but I also know entrepreneurs to be types who always check to make sure no money is left on the table. Grant funding and government clients aren't exactly foreign to the business community, though, since many small businesses contract with the government. Some companies get only the occasional prime contract or subcontract with the feds or a state agency. But it's not uncommon for firms to earn their entire livelihoods from government contracting. An entire industry not unrelated to grant writing is dedicated to contracting. Still, that we choose to do business with the government doesn't matter to us as businesspeople if we feel stymied by regulations and unjustified taxation. It's a fact: Red tape makes entrepreneurs seethe even if they do business with the government. Are we contradicting ourselves? Can we ask for these grant and contracting dollars and yet expect to handle them any way we please? I'm not here to create a judgment on the issue, only to share what I know is available. I

> We do give up some measure of freedom to direct every aspect of a project when we ask another entity for money.

receive compensation directly from companies to advise them on competing for grant funding. So, while I personally don't contract with the government, I indirectly make a living from the existence of grant funding, be it government or nonprofit sourced. Foundations are certainly not without their special and equally limiting criteria and requirements.

Do we contradict ourselves a little when we say that we're concerned about where the government is headed with spending but we wouldn't mind receiving government funding if it were available? Probably. Are we hypocritical when we echo the prevailing disgust with so-called corporate greed and stratospheric CEO compensation, and yet are willing to get our hands on donations by wealthy corporations to their grant-awarding foundations? I'd say we are.

It is not my intention to offer you a judgment or provide a point of view on why grant funding should or should not exist. After eight years in the grant writing industry, I certainly have my opinions, but that is not the value I bring to you in this book. Make your own opinion, but just make it an educated one. If you need help formulating it, and many people who explore grants do, jump ahead to Part Two where I spend several chapters working through the ramifications (positive and negative) of accepting grant dollars.

JUMP AHEAD

For questions and considerations around the ramifications of accepting and using grant funding, see Part Two.

PERSPECTIVES ON PROSPERITY

> Learning is an ornament in prosperity, a refuge in adversity, and a provision in old age.
>
> —*Aristotle*

Despite the interest in new funding sources and the gaining acceptance of unique routes to cash, putting in the effort in gather up the money is still difficult and requires some expertise. For many entrepreneurs, the focus on their concept is what glitters and garnering funding is just another chore. I won't be able to put the polish on the concept of fundraising for you. Unfortunately, grant writing can be a boring topic. However, take this process not only as an essential *but also as a creative portion* of your bigger project. I think the big picture of funding is quite illuminating. The route a concept takes from idea to plan to implementation with a vehicle called *money* makes for an interesting ride. You read in the statistics I presented that as many firms close per year as open—even though the number of new entrepreneurs is blossoming. If you don't want to be on the *closed* statistic list, you've got to apply creativity to this aspect of your business, which is what I encourage with the snapshots in this chapter.

We exist in a time when unique funding sources are the rage. Grants may be one of those for you. But, application preparation can be dull. I think one reason entrepreneurs as a rule don't use grants is that there has been no bridge between the grant writing industry and the financial sector. Nothing has existed to show that this alternative funding source is relevant. When I've read grant writing books I haven't seen any of the what's-in-it-for-me type of material that would motivate anyone to buy into a laborious process. So, I developed my own formula to guide this discussion so we never get off-track. As it turns out, those bits of conversation I shared earlier in the chapter became a process that works.

CHAPTER TWO

The Five Steps to Navigating the Grant Process

> Opening a grant application template and typing up the forms with no plan is like driving a car blindfolded. You need a process.

The tattered scrap of paper read:

"Today I am Potential, tomorrow I am Success."

Looking down at it, I was puzzled. Outside my home office window, the Midwestern January sky appeared like liquid gunmetal. Beneath it, the earth appeared so utterly lifeless, like a vast landscape of clay yet unmolded by a potter's hands. I was sitting at my desk, creatively procrastinating by looking through old writing files and wondering what I was going to do next.

I was the writer of those words some 15 years before, at age 14. Now, having left my job two months before to refocus on my new venture—Aubrey's Natural Meats, LLC, a direct-to-consumer custom beef and pork business—I was bereft of ideas and looking through old snatches of articles, book concepts, and catchy phrases I'd once intended to make something of. I often found myself either looking though my "ideas files" or seated at my 1928 baby-grand piano when I was either utterly lacking or desperately seeking inspiration. I kept looking back at the little quote: "Today I am Potential, tomorrow I am Success." I had even capitalized *Potential* and *Success* as if they were key words to something magnificent. What did this little statement matter? Why did it bother me so much today? I worried that it was the sinking feeling of failure that hung in the room like lead.

Knowing I was meant to be an entrepreneur had never been a problem—clearly I was confident from an early age—knowing how to be a *successful entrepreneur* was the problem. Only eight months into my business venture, my new SBA line of credit was maxed, and I had no other income since I'd left my job the November before. Using my old standby skills, I'd started freelance writing, but trade journal articles didn't help me keep the new business going. I needed to regain that old confidence; more importantly, I needed a unique form of cash. I didn't want to be just potential, not when I had once been so sure I could do more.

If you're wondering if this is how I started into the grant writing business, it is, but not the way you might guess. I have never used a grant for my own businesses, though my eventual grant consulting business started with one initial client—me.

Browsing online led me to grants for small businesses. I'd never considered taking grant assistance. However, that afternoon, I managed to locate a couple of programs that appeared to fit my local foods business project, or so I thought. I finally came to the conclusion that many entrepreneurs reach just before something major happens: *What the heck, why not give this a shot?* So, I applied for two grants. That is initially how I got into the grant writing business.

I didn't win either grant, or even the third grant I applied for later that year. But, as winter gave onto spring, I began to realize a new season of green was sprouting for my business. Grant funding did become a means to a positive end for me, and I'm going to show you how, too. The knowledge I impart in this book was not automatically acquired. I was a poor application preparer in my initial attempts. My first three grants bombed. They didn't meet *all* the criteria for an application train-wreck, but I think they came pretty close (once I began learning what was *really* required).

Although my first three grants bombed, the good thing is that I didn't get paid to write those, find the funding, or consult on how to use the funding. I wrote them for my own business. One of the things that finally got me through the funding funk was that I decided to find out why I had failed at grant preparation. I didn't even plan to work on a grant application for myself again; I still felt compelled to figure out what I'd missed in the process. So, one day, I called the federal governmental agency listed as the contact for the most recent denial letter I'd received.

My first three grants bombed. This book imparts the knowledge from my experience since then as to what's really required to succeed in grant making.

Assuming I'd just get a voice mail, imagine my surprise when a live person answered! After stumbling around a moment, I simply stated my questions:

"I've got my grant denial letter here and I'm sure there is a good reason that I didn't get funded. I'm sure, too, that it's my fault because I really didn't know how to prepare an application for USDA. Could you help me understand what I don't know?"

The exuberance of the woman on the line surprised me yet again. "Sure! I'd be happy to do that!" she began pleasantly. "We get so many applications that have good ideas but are not what we're looking for and then we can't get them to score well," she continued. "Your idea with the meat business sounded interesting, but it just wasn't a defined project."

"Defined project. What do you mean?" I queried.

"Well, that's just it; that is what applicants don't seem to get. It all starts with being able to explain to us what you want in a way that we can see how it would fit the program and the parameters that we have to work with," she went on. "I'd love to have more applications prepared well that we could fund. But my hands are tied; we have to score them with the regulations we are given."

Pausing a moment, still not certain, I said: "I do think I could get better at this if I just understand a bit more of the lingo."

"Yes, we really need people who know how to prepare these and there are so few resources we can refer other applicants to! Why don't you come down to my office and we'll just work through it?" she offered.

Astonished, I agreed immediately.

NEW VENTURES, ENTREPRENEURIAL NEEDS

Entrepreneurs often report experiencing a sense of what I like to call the *knowing*. I could call it *intuition* or maybe just *self-reliance*. In my case, particularly back when my self-confidence was waning as in the earlier story, I think the knowing acts more like a built-in guidance system that provides assurance that despite odds being faced, I'm on the right track. I have no doubt that my fellow entrepreneurs still weigh out choices systematically and evaluate things intelligently, but I'm convinced we do this process differently. One thing I experience that leads me to a decision is reoccurring themes.

Back to my conversations with my kind program manager at USDA, on our second meeting, she brought up the need for grant writing help again.

"We just don't have the capacity to train everyone on how to prepare their applications. Our job is to administer them. Even if you could improve your own work, or just help someone else, it would really help us," she added.

It turns out that, congruent to the accidental education I was obtaining in grant writing, a boom in available grant programs for the areas of renewable energy and agricultural energy development was happening. In the early 2000s, USDA and other agencies started offering more programs to implement rural development projects that were literally happening in my backyard. Living in rural Indiana and being a lifelong farm-girl, I watched with interest. Acquaintances began hearing about funding, but like me, had no guess at how to obtain it. Using grants was utterly foreign to most renewable energy and agricultural project developers back then, though many are working with that source of funding today. My USDA contact shared with me her frustration that she couldn't fund more projects in the state. While my applications hadn't been awarded, either, apparently they weren't deplorable like many she reviewed. In a whispered voice, she said: "I've even received a few filled out in pencil. Can you imagine?"

That there was funding in an industry I understood that no one was going after correctly was intriguing to say the least. That little urge for more information I'd felt a couple of months earlier became a louder voice. Besides these issues, another theme kept coming to me—it was the word, not the concept of, *project*.

"Having a clear project, that's a must, Sarah," said Deb. We were now on a first-name basis. "Project isn't just a description of what the applicant wants to do. It has to be a description of what the applicant wants to do that we want to fund and fits in our guidelines."

The message was getting louder. By fall, Deb had invited me to attend a meeting where the USDA was going to present several grants to anyone interested. They were trying to improve awareness, but outreach wasn't exactly their primary job. I offered to send the notice out to my address book. Word was getting around, my husband, Cary, said, that I was working on grants.

At the meeting, Deb was one of the speakers reviewing the program guidelines. She turned to me and asked what I had learned with the grant applications I'd completed. Off guard, I stood to tell the group that "in my experience" I had learned that everything was about having projects that met the agency's goals while meeting yours. Of the 40 people in attendance, nearly 20 wanted to chat with me afterward. I left there with two clients.

That first year in the grant business I wrote two grants. I won one and lost one. The second year I did 49 grants and won 95 percent of them. Fast forward to the present and over nearly ten years I've now written hundreds of successful grants resulting in millions of dollars headed to clients. How did I begin? I just kept at it. I kept making decisions based upon the feedback from the agencies, always looking at the grant application from the agency's perspective and not my client's. Once I began doing this for a living (I sold the meat business after two seasons in grant consulting) I realized that I made decisions for grant applications in a particular fashion. I also had as many conversations as possible to hone that system and build my experience. This experience ultimately led me to determine there are just five basic areas needed to develop, package, submit, and win a grant. Over time, I've honed these five areas into a system of steps that I call the Prosperity Process©.

OVERVIEW OF THE FIVE-STEP PROCESS

There are books on grant writing, and there are books on business; there are even books that tell you how to start a grant writing business. This book is about how and when you could use grants to get cash to start or expand your business. This is the book the small business financial market has been missing. See Figure 2.1.

In what follows, I'll review each step in general terms to get us started. As the chapters progress, I'll provide examples, including recounting many conversations where I have used the process with clients to achieve their funding objectives.

Please note, for the purposes of this work, I will use the terms *grant agency, funding organization, funder, grant maker,* and others interchangeably. I will also, unless specifically speaking about one or the other, lump all types of funders that I cover in this book, including government, trade association, and foundation, into the same category and use the term I coined for them—*grant funding organizations (GFOs).*

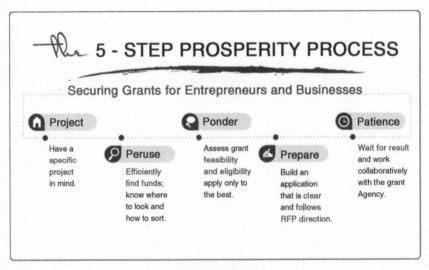

FIGURE 2.1

Five-Step Prosperity Process
Source: Created by Brandrenew.

GRANTS GURU GLOSSARY

GFO (grant funding organization): This is the blanket term used in this book to describe any governmental, trade group, nonprofit, corporate, or charitable foundation or any other organization that awards grant dollars.

Before You Begin: The Idea

The process steps are in order from start to finish. There is probably a Step 1A, which I should note here. The entire process begins with you—it does not begin with the grant agency, or with your team, or by hiring a grant writer. The process begins with an idea. That's one reason that I believe grant funding can work for entrepreneurs— because you as an innovator are comfortable with and perhaps natural at producing unique ideas and implementing them into projects. The best grants are won by a combination of the best ideas that have been packaged correctly. That's really all it takes. Take a look at the path to grant funding I've built in Figure 2.2. We'll be working through this often, so you'll see it again in more detail.

> One reason that I believe grant funding can work for entrepreneurs is because you as an innovator are comfortable with and perhaps natural at producing unique ideas and implementing them as projects.

What's your solid idea? I'll spend plenty of quality time helping you turn that into a project. If you'd like to see how ready you are today, take a look at the Prosperity Project Evaluation tool in Appendix A.

JUMP AHEAD

To gauge your idea's suitability for grant funding today, jump to Appendix A.

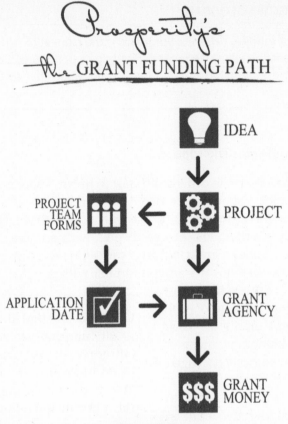

Prosperity's

~~the~~ GRANT FUNDING PATH

FIGURE 2.2

Grant Funding Path
Source: Created by Brandrenew.

Step 1: Project

When LeAnn called to discuss the new technology she and her husband were planning to bring to market, I was interested, but at the end of that phone call, I couldn't figure a way to make the odor-reducing, organically made concoction marketable to a grant agency. It was odd, because usually a good technology (i.e., idea) is a great place to start. It took me a while to realize the issue was clarity and direction. This being early in my grant-preparing-for-hire career, I was still harkening back to the informative USDA employee who had helped me see the mistakes in my early grant applications: "It all comes down to project." I heard the words echoing in my ears like a mantra.

Ultimately, we worked together to build a specific project—that is, a product description that was measureable and had a start and endpoint, and an outcome that the agency cared about—into a useable grant application. LeAnn was able to win a grant for a small business proof-of-concept for $70,000 for the first stage and to apply for a second stage for $150,000.

GRANTS GURU GLOSSARY

Project: For my grant writing purposes, the definition of the word *project* is an activity, work, service, or tangible item that when described is measurable, has a targeted outcome that aligns with the grant funding organization's (GFO's) goals, has designated milestones that are realistic, including a justifiable, workable budget, and demonstrates the ability to stand alone and persist successfully once grant funding is gone and has some aspect of greater good.

After LueAnn's situation and the success we achieved, I began starting each client with a discussion of the concept of *Project*. Here are the key components and a discussion of each.

Measurable. All grant applications must demonstrate that the work being done has measurable components that can be accomplished and reported. These will vary in degree of technicality and detail from program to program, but all good applications demonstrate as much measurability as possible. You will see the remaining project points are all measurable, too. This is by design and should absolutely not be overlooked, though it is simple in nature. Measurements can be hard data, changes realized or implied as a result of your project. They could also be accounted for in the number of participants you enroll and just about anything that can be compared from a before-and-after standpoint.

Targeted Outcome. The grant agency is seeking to award money for a purpose. There are not dollars for those simply needing money without a specific project. Perhaps we call that something else entirely, such as an *aid* program or even an *entitlement* program, but we do not call aid-for-the-sake-of-aid a grant award. Do not mistake this to mean that in applying for a grant you don't have to indicate some need for the funding; you do. However, that need may be financial (example: "The program we are funding is short of cash and cannot continue without additional funding") or it may not be (example: "There are more than x million birds killed each year by X and with funding we can help prevent the loss of the Y breed of bird to extinction").

Grants must accomplish a purpose and you must clearly indicate that your idea, that is, your project, is a solid one by sharing that by awarding funding to it, you will create an outcome that is important and matters to the GFO. I advocate at least three concrete outcomes listed in every grant, though you may need more, particularly if you are working on a very complex project or requesting a great deal of funding.

Finally, some grant programs will require the applicant to indicate that there is a financial need; you must look for each one of these specifically.

Aligns with the GFO's Goals. Fittingly, both this and the targeted outcome seem similar. They are, with one primary distinction. Just because your project meets all the other criteria to be considered a solid project, it is not likely to be a project that a grant agency will fund if you do not explain convincingly how it meets *their* goals. I've had many an entrepreneur argue this point with me, particularly in the case of federal government funding. I wish I had a nickel for every time I heard the line, "Well, my project is so important and will positively affect so many people and create so many jobs that the government will want to/have to be begging to fund it!" I'd truly be pleased with the income, that is, if I took payment in nickels. The thing is, that is incorrect thinking for grant funding. Your project must be both worthwhile and in line with what the grant agency is charged with supporting. Seek the GFO's objectives and then tell them why your project meets those.

Has Designated, Realistic Milestones. These include points in the application and project description as simple as start and endpoint for the funding and completion of the work and possibly as detailed as the specific step-by-step processes employed in a technically complex proof-of-concept. For construction projects, completion of actual work and timelines for ordering equipment, installation, and startup will be paramount. For programming work, the milestones will be centered on developing curriculum and hiring staff or utilizing certain operating expenses. They can be further measured by enrollment in the program funded or the project's eventual ability to move onto a second stage or turn a profit. There is no standard list of milestones for all grants; GFOs will have specifics for which you will need to respond.

Justifiable, Workable Budget. All grants require some kind of budgeting. If you're lucky, this might be as simple as gathering quotes for the work you intend to complete and creating a simple budget of the costs and when you'll be incurring those. In some cases, the budgets can be complex and you will be required to use the GFO's format. I use the term *workable* to mean simply that your budget adds up. *Justifiable* is a more grant-like term. As you may guess, it does mean that you have to provide justification as to how you will use the funding. However, some grants will have detailed budget justification worksheets for completion where there are criteria you are charged with meeting and demonstrating.

Demonstrates Ability to Sustain After Grant Funding.
Finally, a good project must stand alone. All grant funds come to an end. This means that projects must be able to explain their longevity plans

A good project must stand alone. All grant funds come to an end. This means that projects must be able to explain their longevity plans even before they get off the ground even before they get off the ground. Financial projections and income-producing opportunities are likely a way to show this. For programming, future endowments or simply a certain endpoint to the program where dollars being directed at it will cease can be the route to show.

Shows Some Aspect of Greater Good. Even if an application doesn't specifically ask for your mention of the greater accomplishments you can achieve, include it anyway and highlight it well. I always remind applicants that just because they are achieving financial gain from the project does not mean that the agency cares about that fact per se. Realize that the GFO is about awarding concepts, furthering missions, and achieving objectives. Discuss how your project, even though it may be located at your place of business, benefits many.

Step 2: Peruse

Ken stopped me regularly at meetings and events around my home area of Indianapolis. He always had the perfect grant in mind for his project and sought my help in completing an application. The problem was that Ken was spending hours and hours each week trying to find funding, and he was still coming up short.

"I just don't understand how you can even make any money in this business, Sarah," he commented one evening at an industry cocktail reception. "Do you just sit on your computer all day looking through grants.gov?" he said, downing the last of his gin. "That must be awful!"

"No, I use some help to find grants. I do go on the federal websites, but it's not for hours and hours a day," I said with a slight laugh.

"Wow! You must be spending a fortune on staffing, then, or else you're missing all the good grants!" he joked. "There must be a billion programs on there!"

Some of us are guilty of loving the chase even more than the capture. This second step in the process, *Peruse*, is about the hunt for green. You must know where to look. Simply browsing randomly on the Internet, as I once did, and as Ken was wont to do, will get you nowhere. Ken isn't altogether wrong; the sheer number of options available is mind bending, and then sorting them into useable groups is a fulltime job. The key is efficiency in knowing where and how to look. It's also about regularity and using some kind of scheduled approach. I'll share with you my best practices for finding funding and staying current with options that are available for funding. Programs change and program information is often quite a deciphering mess. We'll look into how to do this quickly and create a tracking system.

Step 3: Ponder

Planners and strategizers rejoice! Step 3 is your time to shine, and it's my personal favorite, too. This is the place where you consider the big picture. Call it the overview and the strategic planning step. I think it's so important that I devoted an entire section of this book to this step, *Ponder*. Step 3 is what really separates the good, fundable applications from those good projects that just don't get funded. Step 3 is where I missed the mark when I wrote my first three grants. What's funny is that once I really got it, Step 3 made the most sense.

To summarize: Never apply for a grant for which you are not eligible or that you do not have any hope of receiving due to factors beyond your control.

One thing entrepreneurs are often good at is knowing when to get in and when to get out. We're accustomed to weighing decisions and assessing risk using skills we may have developed in life or in previous corporate jobs. However, from the time we arrive at the doorstep of entrepreneurship, those former skills are immediately dated. You know what I mean. You realize one day that the big strategic plan you authored for the corporation is now too slow and too laborious. It's just not applicable to your current style of moving. You're making decisions on short notice, but not without intelligent consideration because each decision now is made with money from your pocket—money that could alternatively be the family's meal and education money. Or perhaps it's a cashed-in 401(k) you promised yourself was a good idea; or maybe you have been lucky enough to obtain a gift or loan from a friend or benevolent relative.

No, sadly, you did not write the grant regulation. Nor are you the grant reviewer who will score and bequeath your award. So, in light of both of these startling developments, you have but one recourse: Be eligible and be prudent. Apply only for those grants where the fit is good.

Here's the caveat that I'll provide some context to later on: You will never fit perfectly. *Uh-oh.* I just contradicted myself.

No, actually, not, instead of being contradictory here, I just offered an extremely valuable tip. Just as marriage isn't perfect but rather takes work and no day is ever perfect, even award-garnering grant applications never fit perfectly into all the grant agency guidelines. So, you've got to adjust and be willing to give and take to make your project fit within the regulations and terms of eligibility. If you cannot adjust—and there are a lot of good reasons to say no—walk away, it's as simple as that.

Step 4: Prepare

My husband, Cary Aubrey, and I have a small cattle farm. We both enjoy this business and work hard at in our own ways. I am the strategizer who puts thought into where the market is going and how soon we need to adjust to meet demands. Cary likes to talk about that, too, but he tires of it quicker than I do. He just likes to get his work done, call it a day, go to bed early, and hit it hard again in the morning. He is a task-oriented guy who at 47 can work faster than three teenaged boys after pretty girls.

Every single morning, he starts the day by saying the same thing to me: "Well, I'm going to go feed." As of this writing, we've been married over 13 years. Every day he has told me that he will rise from bed and go feed cows. Never has there been a day that he has forgotten to feed the cows. Should he ever fail to feed the cows (this won't ever happen, of course, but . . .) the cows would promptly remind us, anyway, with irritated bellowing and general stomping around the barn lot. So, if he did get somehow off course (this will never happen, of course), animals that require eating daily have a built-in reminder system called hunger. But, we don't need that little reminder alarm. All we need is Cary—the supreme master of getting work done!

For all you Carys out there, you fine, upstanding task-oriented folks, this is your preferred step. You will absolutely excel at this important step—*Prepare*.

I believe most of the other grant books have been written by the Cary Aubreys of the world because most of the other processes for successful grant accumulation focus almost entirely around the actions associated with preparing the application. True, one of the biggest reasons (not *the* biggest, though!) that grants don't receive funding is poor application quality. So, we will focus an entire section of this book on making sure that you are looking for the key areas that make up a solid application.

Step 5: Patience

"Are we there yet?" How many parents have heard that one?

How many fellow grant writers have heard it with this twist: "Have we received our check yet?"

Before heading too much farther into this book, let's begin with a fact: If you have not heard whether you received your grant, then you do not know whether you received your grant.

That sounds obvious. However, I know many entrepreneurial clients that really struggle with the wait times common to grant funding. Timing is the number-one reason I suggest certain prospects avoid using grant funding in the first place. Not everyone can handle the wait.

Update for those who are certain the world revolves around them: If no one has convinced you of the fallacy of these facts before now, just apply for a federal grant, and then try to convince the grant agency to move the thing forward on your timeline, and you'll realize, tragically, that the world does not in fact revolve around your schedule. *Patience* is important in the grant funding process. The above comments were meant to be self-deprecating since I've tried to hurry GFOs along when clients pressured me. I learned, and you will, too. We are at the mercy of someone else when we request money through this process. Patience comes in the form of waiting, sometimes months or maybe even more than a year or two if you have to reapply, but also in the form of compliance. Often, once we turn in an application our next step is not checking our PayPal account for extra cash (I don't believe most grants award through PayPal, anyway). You may be back and forth answering questions with the grant agency for a while. This can seem irksome to many entrepreneurs. I understand this, but this stage is the turn to the backstretch, so patience must be harnessed if you want to use grants.

PERSPECTIVES ON PROSPERITY

> If we had no winter, the spring would not be so pleasant: if we did not sometimes taste of adversity, prosperity would not be so welcome.
> —*Anne Bradstreet, British poet*

As I stated at the beginning of this chapter, opening a grant application template and typing up the forms with no plan is like driving a car blindfolded. You need a process. Certainly, a quick overview of the five essential steps is just the beginning, but by now you have a feel for the format I'll use to guide you through building a solid grant strategy and a successful grant application. My steps don't have to be completed in order, though I find moving in the sequence *project-peruse-ponder-prepare-patience* is the most common route most applicants take. It's true that idea is always first, and in my experience, following idea, project is best worked through second. If you cannot clearly articulate the project, your subsequent searching and feasibility analysis will be only so-so.

Besides sharing my process and describing the steps, the other takeaway from this chapter is to point out that there really is a good deal of pre-work involved long before a grant application is ever typed or submitted—much less awarded. The investment in the solid, strategic initial planning is what separates the grant winners from the also-rans.

Grant funding is not necessarily the easiest row to hoe to unearth cash. As with Ms. Bradstreet's quote, I concur that we cannot see how far we've come until we've had to work for it. So, it seems free money is not free, but it certainly can be worth the effort!

CHAPTER THREE

What Is a Grant?

There are grants, loans, credits, rebates, entitlements, and more. Keeping them straight takes definitions.

Bernie had been calling me nearly every day for almost two weeks. In part because I really felt bad for him, I usually took his calls. But, I couldn't help Bernie. His business was in foreclosure and he thought maybe a grant or some bailout money would heal his wounds and patch his small manufacturing company back together.

Bernie explained to me during his first call that he planned to make solar panels and the components needed to install them. At first glance, I thought perhaps there could be something there with the grant programs I was using at the time in renewable energy. We talked a while and as the call progressed, it turned out that Bernie wasn't hoping to *start* that process; rather, he was in the "dream stage," but had no real plans or technology or business partners to begin his work. What he had was a closed factory that had struggled to meet payroll for the last several years and had finally shut down. He'd read that solar, wind, and other renewables were the wave of the future and was certain that everyone was getting grants to get into that business. He wanted me to apply for a grant that would help him enter the market, too. While it's easy to dream up an idea, it's not possible to win a grant with no more readiness than that.

"But the federal government bailed out GM and the other auto companies!" Bernie exclaimed.

"I realize that; however, this situation is not the same," I countered yet again, weakly.

"Well, we bailed out the banks. Was that a big grant program, or what?" Bernie asked, honestly. He was not being trite; the coverage of these bailouts made it seem as though there was an application process where anyone could fill one out and pull a business out of failure.

"It's not exactly how it works, Bernie. I'm sorry. I cannot explain all the details of TARP, it's not my area of expertise," I said, hoping that would suffice, but feeling it might not.

"You're a grant writer and you don't even know that?" he said, irritated.

"No, I'm afraid I don't. What those companies received wasn't like most grants."

"What is it then? I guess I'm not 'too big to fail,'" he said in disgust.

I really felt for Bernie, but I couldn't help and he couldn't accept it. I was not able to be Bernie's rainmaker and neither was the grant funding process.

Hopefully, you're not surprised to learn that grants certainly cannot do it all. While the concept of receiving "money for nothing" is alluring, you know by now that it's not true. Grants don't save businesses in foreclosure from becoming empty storefronts, though there are ways to use grant funds to expand business operations. In this chapter, I want to get very specific about the types of things grants can help with and what they cannot. You need to know the answers, and though this chapter is a bit of a definition and a lesson, I believe the information here is extremely important for entrepreneurs. Most grant books give you the how-to-write-a-narrative, but they don't explain when a grant can and cannot help you. That's why this chapter appears early in my book. I know it contains quite a few definitions, but I hope this chapter can save you time and frustration as well as giving you ideas you never thought could fit.

The federal government defines a grant as follows: "Grants are not benefits or entitlements. A federal grant is an award of financial assistance from a federal agency to a recipient to carry out a public purpose of support or stimulation authorized by a law of the

United States. Federal grants are not federal assistance or loans to individuals."[1]

This definition can be found by browsing the government's massive grant clearinghouse and funding announcement depository, www.grants.gov. However, while this definition is accurate to the federal government's position of grants, it's not complete when looking at the total grant funding picture as we are exploring it in this book. So, I decided to put together my own definition of the word *grant* as it applies to funding for entrepreneurs.

What follows in this chapter is my personal definition of what a grant is and is not. I built a definition and I will deconstruct it into the elements of a grant. This section is meant for clarification about what types of funding sources make up grant dollars, and also to explain which funding sources are not grants at all—though they may appear to be like cousins in the same branch of the family. Read this chapter carefully and consider referring back to it when you come across funding opportunity announcements where the lines blur between grants, loans, rebates, and tax credits. Don't worry— these are all compared and dissected in this chapter.

BRINGING STRUCTURE TO THE GRANT PROCESS

I often speak to groups that tell me they already know all they need to know about "what a grant is," but once we've dialogued a bit, I am willing to push them on that. Grants are not just free money or a gift you don't have to return. We are talking about a business transaction, not a windfall from your benevolent grandparents. A better understanding of what grants are, and are not, and what they can, and likely cannot, accomplish helps your searching, applying, and chances of receiving *greatly*. It also reduces expectations that will

> In order to obtain a grant, your needs have to align with the funder's (GFO's) goals and limitations.

---

1. www.grants.gov/aboutgrants/jsp.

never come true and will teach you to apply for *only those programs* that best match your business needs and the grant maker's objectives.

The first way to determine how to align your grant with the funder's goals and limitations is to start with a specific, measurable project, as you learned in Chapter 2.

A project must include:

- A clearly stated purpose or objectives and desired outcomes as a result of doing the project
- Clear, achievable milestones
- A timeline to start and complete
- A budget (if there are cost quotes, all the better)

It also:

- Must be relevant to the type of work the agency wants to fund
- Must have a budget that is clear and is explained to the agency
- Must be somehow tied to the greater good

You need to understand how to show them what you want. No matter what the work or request is, it's still a project (see Figure 3.1). I'll explain in the balance of the chapter by showing you what grants are and are not.

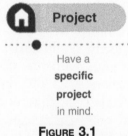

FIGURE 3.1

Project

Source: Created by Brandrenew.

THE ELEMENTS OF A GRANT

In nearly every speech that I give on the topic of grant funding, I start with this section by describing the role of grants. Even with experienced audiences, I have found that most people—even professionals who have applied for grants in the past—really don't understand them. Rather, it seems there is a certain mystique around grant funding. I'm convinced that sometimes people inquire about my services because they believe we are the keepers of some special secrets that unlock the keys to cash. Yes, understanding how to navigate the world of grants and funding agencies takes some practice and learning. There are trade secrets that I've developed over time to help my applications be more successful than those of a novice. In reality, though, the concept of grants and grant making is not all that complicated. It becomes complicated when the agency or foundation imposes its views and desires upon a process. You see, foundations through the missions of their agendas and desires of private donors influence every aspect of the application process. Government operates within "required" red tape, taking the intentions of well-meaning legislators and drilling those down into grant lingo and confusing things called *federal registers* where grant programs are announced. All this then boils down to hundreds of forms and account numbers. Navigating these factors is a fulltime job.

Top-Six Items that Define a Grant:
1. Award of cash money

2. Not required to be repaid

3. Funds for use with a specified purpose

4. Funds to be used in a specified timeframe

5. Subject to compliance and a grant agreement

6. Competitively awarded

The quickest way to explain this is to begin with my definition of a grant: A grant is the award of cash money to an individual, company, municipality, or organization that does not have to be repaid by the awardee to the beneficing agency, donor, or foundation. The grant money is tied to specified terms formally agreed upon between the benefactor and the awardee. Grant funds must be used for a specified purpose during a specified timeframe. Grant funds are often distributed on a reimbursement basis with the awardee paying for all or a portion of the project before receiving dollars from the benefactor agency. Grants require reporting to the benefactor on the use of funds in the form of actual results or in validation that the money was used for the agreed-upon purpose. Grants can be recalled from the benefactor agency for noncompliance and even be required to be repaid for noncompliance.

This being a rather long definition, it is important to clarify it in detail. In what follows, I break out this definition into six parts.

Award of Cash

I'll begin with everyone's favorite part of the definition: "A grant is the award of cash money to an individual, company, municipality, or organization that does not have to be repaid by the awardee to the benefactor agency, donor, or foundation."

Award in cash: When you win a grant, you will be receiving a check or, more than likely today, a direct deposit into your checking account. While some philanthropic organizations offer to provide free services, training, or other incentives such as tax abatements, those items do not meet the definition of the word *grant* for the purposes of this resource. The applicant then has the discretion (within the terms of the grant agreement) to purchase the items or services noted in the application with that cash. Grants, therefore, do allow some flexibility in terms of the vendors and services selected by the awardee. Entrepreneurs will appreciate that grants do not require them to patronize a certain set of approved vendors. The money usually passes through, in cash, from the awardee (you) to the vendor you ultimately select for the desired work.

This means that you will likely be the one sending the payment to your vendors from the grant funding you received.

No repayment: Grants are not required to be repaid and thus should not be seen as loans or other kinds of assistance requiring interest payments, fees, or other return of amounts awarded. Assuming compliance with terms of the grant agreement (more on that later), grants are free of charge once awarded.

Type of entity: Another component of this first sentence gives a clue about who is eligible to receive a grant, and the answer is nearly any business, philanthropic, or governmental structure. Governmental agencies give grants to other governmental agencies, just as foundations give grants to other foundations, trade associations award dollars to other trade associations, and all of these groups could potentially give money to businesses, not-for-profits, foundations, corporations, municipalities, and even individuals. Money passes between federal, state, and local governments and between domestic and international foundations. I have had many entrepreneurs tell me that grants are a waste of their time because "there are no grants for businesses." That is simply not true.

Rather than ask the question, "Can a business receive a grant?" ask, "What is the business doing that a GFO might want to award and what grant agencies are awarding grants for the project my business is doing?"

Harkening back to the Five-Step Process, this is the key to Step 1 (Project).

Terms and Timeframe

Terms and timeframe concern the following: "The grant money is tied to specified terms formally agreed upon between the benefactor and the awardee. Funds will be used for a specified purpose during a specified timeframe."

Money is tied to the terms and an agreement: It's this part of the definition where you should seek counsel, if needed, *beyond your grant writer's expertise.* The grant agreement is a legal contract and not one to be taken lightly. Once selection has been made and you receive a letter from the funder that you have been awarded, you'll receive a detailed agreement outlining terms of the program and your reporting requirements. I have many clients who like to skim through this and get right to the check. That is a bad idea. This agreement, and the terms you agree to by accepting it, is your gateway to the funds. Understanding the grant agreement is more important than a quality application because a grant application is simply a proposal. It's a collection of ideas, quotes, and concepts; however, until it reaches the agreement stage, *it is not a promise.*

Knowing the terms and how you must adhere to them is critical. Not fully understanding them is a great way to forgo your funding due to accidental noncompliance.

Funds are used for specified purpose: Again, during the grant application phase, you are proposing a project. Once you get to grant agreement, that proposal turns into a plan. For example, if you apply for grant dollars to complete a new energy efficiency improvement on your site, you cannot additionally buy a new fleet truck even if you think "Well, this truck gets better gas mileage, so it must be considered energy efficient, and I can use grant dollars for it."

No way will that fly. In the grant application and the subsequent grant agreement, the exact purposes for the grant funds have been agreed upon. Changing those terms without prior authorization from the GFO is a great way to jeopardize your grant award. Don't assume how funds are used is open to your interpretation.

GRANTS GURU GLOSSARY

Grant agreement: The grant agreement specifies the terms, timing, and purpose of your approved funding request. What you are able to do with the dollars is delineated in this agreement.

Once you receive an award you are basically locked into doing the work you specified in the application. This is very important. Your GFO may not pay agreed-upon costs if the final invoices for equipment or reports for completed work do not match with the proposal. Do not get yourself caught in this position of jeopardizing your grant award or, worse yet, having bought something you cannot pay for without the grant funds and then finding out the funds will not pay for it.

> Once you receive an award you are basically locked into doing the work you specified in the application.

Are There Ever Any Exceptions? Yes, but I would counsel you not to plan on them. Still, here's one that comes to mind: It is possible to change some of the specified scope of work once the agreement is signed. If you do think you need to change something, speak with your grant agency representative directly, and always get his approval in writing. Obtain that written approval before proceeding. This is not a good place to do something without knowing for certain it is allowed and hope for forgiveness later.

Funds are used during a specified timeframe: Similar to the concept in the previous section discussing purpose and use of funds, when you sign the grant agreement, that proposed timeline from your application becomes carved in stone in the view of the GFO. This is not to punish you. Often, the timeline terms are set because the GFO knows the money must be spent by a certain deadline or they literally won't have it available anymore. This is particularly common when dealing with government funds. Funding for grants is legislated, and legislation changes, earmarks come and go. Knowing that, the agency knows it only has a certain amount of time to implement programs and disperse the funds before they quite literally disappear. Once you realize this, it should incentivize rather than incense you. So, as you approach the grant process, understand when the money must be used and decide whether your project can be completed during that time. If you cannot complete the work and the agency does not or cannot grant you an extension, you will lose the balance of any undrawn funds.

Are There Ever Any Extensions? *Caveat:* Sometimes you can update the schedule and extend the grant, but I caution you not to push this area. Again, speak directly with the grant agency representative, and sign off on a new agreement with new timeline terms. Do not accept a verbal approval from the agency! Get everything in writing, and get it signed by the director of the agency, if possible, or at least the program manager or administrator of the grant program. The word of someone is absolutely not going to cut it if you are later called out and forced to provide validation for that extension.

REMINDER

This goes beyond the definition of a grant, but bears mentioning here. In many cases you cannot start the project before you receive the grant award. It may be several months before you receive notification of award after you submit. Always understand these terms before submitting an application.

Grants Are Usually a Reimbursement

This part concerns the following: "Grant funds are often distributed on a reimbursement basis with the awardee paying for all or a portion of the project before receiving any payment from the benefactor agency."

Reimbursement: Your grant funds are usually not sent until all or a portion of your project is complete.

I know I have just shattered some hopes for a few readers, but, again, I reiterate my claim that the definition of a grant is the best place to start in the grant obtaining process.

In most cases, you do your work, buy your equipment, make your upgrades, or initiate your program and then you will receive dollars from the grantor to pay you back. In some cases, particularly those where the grant is for administrative funds or programmatic work, you may receive a portion of the funds up front to begin the process. In my experience, this is more common with not-for-profits and universities than it is for grants given to for-profit entities.

Pay for all or part of the project: As grants are often dispersed as reimbursement, you will have to show that the required portion has been paid for, or, at the very least, invoiced by the vendor before receiving the funds. So, you need access to funds to cover those costs and allow you to proceed with the project before the cash from the grant arrives in your bank account. The funding for this portion of the project not covered by the grant request is called *matching funds.* In your application, documentation of where the match will come from is required.

GRANTS GURU GLOSSARY

Matching funds: Matching funds are those dollars needed to complete the project that are not included in the grant request. These dollars can be provided by you, your lender, your investors, or possibly even another grant program. In many cases they can also be in any combination of these other funding sources.

Reporting Is Required

This part covers reporting requirements: "Grants require reporting to the benefactor agency showing actual results or in terms of written validation that the money was used for the agreed-upon purpose."

Grants require reporting: Your relationship with the GFO doesn't necessarily end when you receive the direct deposit. I have never worked with a grant that did not require some sort of follow-up reporting. This is especially true with federal grants but it is often required by private or public foundations. Charitable foundations must demonstrate that they correctly administer and spend their dollars to maintain their nonprofit status, so they need your proof of acceptable use of funds.

Reporting need not be intimidating. It can be fairly simple, possibly only required once as a closeout for the grant. Or it can be detailed and regular (such as monthly or quarterly). Many grants will require reports be filed for up to three or even four years post–grant award. Ask for the schedule of the required reporting and make certain there is a person responsible for meeting those timeframes. Also, expect to validate how the funds were used for the specified purpose from the application.

> Your relationship with the GFO doesn't necessarily end when you receive the direct deposit.

Grants Can Be Recalled

This portion discusses how you could lose your grant: "Grants can be recalled from the benefactor agency for noncompliance and even be required to be repaid for noncompliance."

WHAT IS A GRANT?

Grants recalled for noncompliance: What do I mean by grants being recalled for noncompliance? Hopefully your project does run smoothly, but there are a number of factors post–grant agreement that can leave your grant promise empty. Usually, I see this type of noncompliance when a project cannot get started or reach completion. Examples of this include situations where no permitting or zoning can be obtained for a site improvement or when equipment cannot be obtained, designed, or built in a timely fashion and a suitable replacement cannot be identified. Basically, a grant award recalled for noncompliance means that you can't prove to the GFO's liking that your work is still eligible or that your progress remains on schedule.

Caveat: I have seen situations where compliance problems were beyond the awardee's control. Usually, there is a provision for appeal, so inquire about it, if needed.

Required to be repaid: You read that correctly: A grant might be required to be repaid for noncompliance. *Disclaimer:* I have never had this happen to one of my clients and have not been involved in a situation where a grant agency actually asked the awardee to return funds. But, it can and does happen. If you report accurately, report timely, and use funds correctly, expect no problems.

A Grant Is Always Competitive

The final part includes one major defining factor—competition: "Grants are competitively awarded."

Grants are competitively awarded: I define grants differently from other assistance because they are not guaranteed to be won, even if the application is done perfectly. An applicant can be qualified to receive a grant, be eligible, meet all the criteria, and still not win. This fact is often one that entrepreneurs struggle to accept.

WHAT GRANTS ARE *NOT*

As you have just read, I use a very detailed definition of the word *grant* in my consulting practice. I do use each of the previously mentioned segments when talking to any new prospect after approaching grant funding as part of the their business financial

■ 42 ■

model. If you stayed with me as I completely dissected my own definition, then I ask you to hang on a bit longer and finish out this chapter by discussing what grants are not.

Top Items Not *Included in Definition of a Grant:*
1. Loans
2. Scholarships
3. Rebates
4. Tax credits
5. Endowments or revolving funds
6. The same as other fundraising activities
7. *Free* money

Grants versus Loans

It is important to note a couple of things here that you will see occasionally associated with grants that may confuse the issue of grants verses loans.

You may see loan guarantees associated with grant programs, possibly even tied to a grant program through what is a called a *combination application* or possibly as a part of the funding announcement for the grant. The two are still separate and can usually be applied for as two separate applications, or can be applied for together in a combination. I work with a USDA program that offers this possibility every year. There have even been cases when points and scoring are affected by whether the grant is applied for by itself or in combination with the loan guarantee. If you do see a loan guarantee from a grant agency, that does not make it synonymous with the grant, but it may be another incentive to consider.

Most people are familiar with the Small Business Administration (SBA) and the fact that SBA loans exist through your banking institution. What you may not realize, however, is that it is not the bank offering a guarantee to you. Rather, the guarantee, offered through the U.S. government, goes to the bank protecting them against your default on the loan. In his 2011 revision of his 1999 book, *The SBA Loan Book*, author Charles S. Green provides an excellent, detailed guide to these commonly used loan guarantees. He writes that more than 50,000 entrepreneurs have used his book to learn about SBA loans.

Green mentions the two major programs from SBA for loan guarantees, the 504 Loan Program and the 7(a) Loan Guaranty Program, and a succinct definition:

> The 7(a) program is SBA's primary loan program for helping startup businesses, providing funds for a variety of general business purposes. SBA does not make direct loans. Instead, it provides a credit-enhancement to participating lending institutions in the form of a long-term loan guaranty.[2]

Green goes on to point out that in the case of SBA, the guarantee is offered to the lender at up to 75 percent of the total loan amount up to $2 million. He mentions that small loans, those $250,000 and less, are guaranteed up to 80 percent.

The SBA is not the only governmental entity to offer loan guarantees; they are often issued in relationship to other funding incentives like grants and even tax credit–type programs. But, they are not grants. Here's my definition of a loan guarantee:

GRANTS GURU GLOSSARY

Loan guarantee: A loan guarantee is a guarantee to a lender from the government that the lender will be repaid a portion of the amount lent to a qualified borrower in the event that the borrower defaults on the loan. The entire loan amount borrowed is not guaranteed; usually guarantees run between 25 and 80 percent of the amount borrowed. The guarantee will not go to the borrower and the borrower does not receive cash for the guarantee. The lender is charged a fee by the government for accepting the guarantee and that fee, usually around 1 to 4 percent, is passed on to the borrower.

---

2. Charles S. Green, *The SBA Loan Book: The Complete Guide to Getting Financial Help through the U.S. Small Business Administration* (Avon, MA: Adams Media, 2011), 2.

Grants versus Scholarships

Scholarships may seem a bit like grants but I separate them because scholarships do not have, in my view, the legal and financial ramifications of grants. For example, you will likely not sign an agreement to receive a scholarship as you will with most grants. Grants and scholarships both might be returned if they are not used properly, but the due diligence behind the reporting requirements and specificity of using scholarship money is nowhere near the level of accepting grant funding.

Grants versus Rebates

Rebates are akin to refunds in that they are a return of a portion of the amount you already paid. Rebates are not competitive and that is one way I distinguish them from grants. At least until the dollars run out, anyone who qualifies (meaning, is eligible for) should expect to receive the refund offered by the rebate program.

Grants versus Tax Credits

Grants are not tax credits. As you know, grants are awards of cash. Tax credits do not imply that you will receive a payment directly, nor that the payment be competitive. A tax credit, quite simply, is an opportunity for a deduction from a person or business's tax liability owed to a state or federal agency, as defined by the *Oxford English Dictionary*.

Grants versus Endowments

Some people believe grants and endowments are the same. I do not. *Endowments* are vehicles to perpetuate funds for a long time. A grant is not an endowment because grants will presumably come to an end much quicker. Federal grants are typically written to sunset after a certain number of years pass or an amount of earmarked funding is exhausted. I usually cannot guarantee that a grant program I used one year will be back the next (though in many cases I'm fairly certain) unless some kind of baseline funding has been enacted so that the program lasts longer than one session to the next. Grants from foundations may come from endowment funds set aside to support activities the foundation desires, but as the grant itself is not the endowment, the grant program may or may not be changed or deleted. Finally, grants, once received by the awardee, do not last for perpetuity. Grants will be available to the awardee only for a certain amount of time, as specified in the agreement. Further, once the grant funds are drawn and the grant is used and closed out, it is not automatically available to the awardee again. The awardee does not automatically re-up with a grant. If available, the awardee would have to reapply. Sometimes, once you've received funding in a specific grant program, you cannot be awarded again for a number of years or ever.

Grants versus Fundraising

I like to mention this point because many people have asked me if I am a fundraising executive. I don't consider that title exactly correct. Yes, I am in business to aid organizations in locating cash in a unique way, but my job is not all-inclusive in the fundraising realm. Besides, I think fundraising is an activity with many facets, with grants being just one aspect of fundraising. Thus, *fundraising is* a verb. The word *grant* is a noun; it is a thing that may or may not be in a larger fundraising package.

Grants Are Not Free Money

I'll say it again: Grants are not free. For the sake of finality, that is the one big takeaway you should leave with after reading this chapter defining what I believe a grant is and is not. You're probably getting the point that a lot of work goes into the process of understanding what is and what is not and how and where to use grant funding. Quite clearly, then, you can now understand why I always laugh at the "I'd like some of that free money, Ma'am" callers I get every few months. While you don't have to pay it back, it's not going to be easy or even cheap to obtain. If you're still up for looking into this funding, follow me into the conversation we'll have around the strategy.

PERSPECTIVES ON PROSPERITY

(prosperity, n.) The condition of being prosperous, successful, or thriving; good fortune, success, well-being, wealth.

—*Oxford University Press*, OED *online*

Having worked through the definition of *grant* throughout this chapter, I thought I would include the Oxford University Press definition from the *OED* online.

Certainly, one can define words like *grant* quite broadly or quite specifically, as I have done in the chapter. *Prosperity* is much the same. Many people think prosperity means to have wealth, but I like the definition of it that points to wealth as one of the synonyms of the word, yet adds other conditions as defining factors, too. So, it seems prosperity is an all-encompassing word. I think prosperity includes a variety of elements of good fortune (as aforementioned), including financial stability, success, and good health.

The key learning in this chapter centers around taking notice. You will begin to learn that definitions, interpretations, and very specific guidelines are the norm in the grant funding business. To be successful in achieving these dollars, you must read very carefully and possibly take some educated guesses at the intent behind the GFO's guidelines. This is why knowing exactly what grants are—and are not—is such an important feature to master early in the process.

The world of using grant funding is like this definition. There are many options, and they do not simply include using government money or being an academic researcher. Grant funding encompasses a great breadth of options for the potential applicant.

CHAPTER FOUR

Is There *Really* Money Out There?

To figure out where to focus your time, you've got to understand the market. Take a good look at the funders.

The opening act with most would-be grant applicants starts something like this:

PROSPECTIVE CLIENT: Is there really any money out there? I mean, it's all been used up by now, right?

CONSULTANT: Yes, there is money, but you have to know where to look. Tell me about your needs. What do you have in mind?

PROSPECTIVE CLIENT: Hold on. Are you really sure this is worth my time? I can't pursue a funding strategy that is going nowhere. Is there anything left after the stimulus money dried up?

CONSULTANT: Absolutely, there are dollars out there, before and since the so-called "stimulus" that made the news. Let's look at the size of the market and I'll explain.

Grants always invite living conversations. Everyone has an opinion on the topic, whether it's about corporate ethics or which political party is in (or out) of office. A regular refrain from both sides of the aisle is that grant funding availability will surely dry up when one or the other party takes over the White House, the State House, the County Seat, the boardroom seat, or the corner office on Wall Street. Everyone is sure someone's going to do away with grant funding entirely. That's bunk. Grants can be political (*are* political), but so is everything. It's time to get over that aspect and move on to opportunity.

Grants are funded by governmental agencies at state and federal levels, and are awarded by corporations and foundations. Grants are even offered by trade groups and associations—maybe even those of which you are a member (or might be considering joining).

MATCHING YOUR PROJECT WITH THE GFOs

To best match your project with the GFOs, start by understanding a little about them. There may be several types of funders issuing notices that read like a fit. But, upon closer examination you might realize that they often do not award the type or amount of funding you need. Let's take a look at the three major categories of grant funding organizations (GFOs):

1. Government
2. Association/trade
3. Foundations and nonprofits

These can be further broken down into:

- Federal government
- State government
- Trade association
- Charitable foundation
- Corporate foundation

There are additional possible combinations of GFOs but for our purposes, we will work through the big three.

Is There Enough Grant Money?

Once you notice something you want—like a new car or a handbag in a certain brand and color—it suddenly seems to appear on every street or slung over every shoulder. If you get into the grant searching arena, it will appear as though *everybody* is applying for grants. I call it the new trend of the mid-2000s. Still, with all the consolidating, budget cutting, and sequestering going on, prospects ask me every day: "Is there enough money left to mess with in this market?"

Programs come and go, some open and others sunset. Because grant programs are well known for being funded sometimes and unavailable others, many people often think the grant funding arena is a fickle avenue for business funding. At the very least, using grants in business planning can be scary for would-be applicants because they likely don't understand the 'world of grant funding' and as such their expectations are all over the board. Some prospects come to me believing they will get all of their project needs met by grant funding, which I caution them is quite unlikely while others believe applying for grants is a waste of time because there is no money available or because winning grants is so competitive the odds are against them. I don't believe it is either of these. My advice is to search the market specific to your project and determine the true potential of funding out there—it will be more for some than others.

The grant marketplace, federal, trade, and foundation, is still a deep well. Later, we'll discuss the *how*, but for now, let me explain the *how much*.

How Big Is the Federal Grant Marketplace?

The federal market for grant funding is big—really big. About 25 federal agencies offer grants to businesses. This represents over 900 different grant agencies or programs that hand out $350 billion annually. The actual number of grant funding opportunities within these 900 different programs is practically limitless—or will certainly seem that way if you ever venture onto grants.gov. Table 4.1

TABLE 4.1 Total Federal Spending on Grants per Fiscal Year

Year	Number of Grants	Total Spending
2013	219,925	$312,949,186,533
2012	500,017	$537,646,104,836
2011	539,320	$567,890,169,349
2010	651,514	$614,386,875,225
2009	579,574	$664,942,955,171
2008	394,901	$419,535,664,223

Source: "Prime Award Spending Data," USASpending.gov. Last modified May 9, 2013, www
.usaspending.gov.

provides a breakout by year as tracked by the website www
.usaspending.gov.

These being the most recent numbers I could obtain, I'll comment on a few current trends. First, the $350 billion annually I called
an average per year is noticeably higher in recent years prior to 2013.
Many of you will have already guessed the cause: The uptick in
2009–2012 numbers is due in part to the "stimulus" that is the
American Reinvestment and Recovery Act (ARRA) funding. By
2013, most of those programs had completed their big rollouts
and were drawing to a close. Where will funding levels go now?
I can't say, but what I can tell you is that there certainly are trends
that remain hot. Check out Chapter 6 for more about that.

JUMP AHEAD

Jump Ahead to Chapter 6 to get an idea of hot funding areas I see right
now.

GOVERNMENT GRANTS

Federal grants are offered through various government agencies.
These programs result from legislation and are mostly funded
through your tax dollars in one way or another. They may come
directly from taxation or other indirect means. Always realize that
governmental grants are funded with our money.

In most cases, the actual design and programmatic options such as eligibility, timelines, required forms, documentation needed, and so on are completed by staff at the governmental agency. Grant administrative staff people are most likely not political appointees, although certainly appointed agency heads will be reviewing new and existing programs and even offering comments or perhaps drafting sections.

Speaking of comments, many grant programs offer what is called a *comment period*. A comment period is a specified time when anyone in the public can literally provide comments to the grant agency. The comment period is always published in the *Federal Register*, a daily publication that lists the thousands of various pending activities, regulations, grant announcements, grant award announcements, comment periods, and numerous other federal government happenings of interest to the public. The website www.regulations.gov is an excellent resource for viewing federal activities and formally submitting comments for open periods. The website defines a *comment* as follows: "A written expression of an opinion or attitude by a member of the public to a government agency about a rulemaking or other action. A date range exists during which an individual can submit a comment."

> Federal tax dollars are most likely the origin of grants offered by the federal government.

GRANTS GURU GLOSSARY

Comment period: A written expression of an opinion or attitude by a member of the public to a government agency about a rulemaking or other action. A date range exists during which an individual can submit a comment.

The federal governmental agency then administers the program. This administration includes finalizing the grant program's rules and requirements, handling the writing of and issuing of announcements, managing the deadlines and handling the questions that come up during the *request-for-proposal* (RFP) period, and scoring the grant applications once received. Sometimes, private sector professionals work with governmental agencies to score grant applications. These professionals may or may not be paid for this work, and they may work independently or in a committee environment. Finally, the governmental agency handles the grant agreement and works with you to distribute payment, should you win the grant. If you do not receive funding and have a question or concern, you will work with the governmental agency. If your grant denial situation requires a conflict resolution, such as in the case of filing an appeal, your mediator may or may not be a governmental employee.

JUMP AHEAD

To learn about appeals and other post-application situations, see Chapter 11.

The Difference between State and Federal Government Grant Makers

Grants offered from state governments are much the same with the exception that many state programs are simply trickle-down programs of the federal government where the state agency becomes the administrator for the federal agency. In that case, it is really still a federal program in my view, although you may be scored at the state level, which can be either a benefit or a drawback, depending largely on your relationship

Grants from state governments either originate as federal dollars—from your tax dollars—that are administered by state agencies or come from individual state tax revenues from a variety of sources within that state. These revenues are used at the state's individual discretion and are not earmarked or matched by federal dollars.

(or lack of one) with that state agency. We'll work through this in more detail in the strategy section of this book, Part Two, beginning with Chapter 5.

JUMP AHEAD

For more information about strategic considerations for using grants, jump ahead to Part Two, beginning with Chapter 6.

State agencies offer their own unique programs, too. These are often funded using state-collected tax revenues. For example, in our home state of Indiana, we fund a grant program for Diesel Emission Reduction through our Department of Environmental Management (IDEM). The program offers approximately $200,000. When revenues are down, the program has fewer dollars to invest or the program is simply not offered that round. Fluctuations such as these are quite common.

How Much Grant Funding Is at the State Level?

The amount of funding available at the state level is harder to compartmentalize as I mentioned previously. Also, I should note that some of the money you saw in the federal chart, Table 4.1, would be transferrable to this state agency chart. Yes, the federal government allocates and awards funding directly to states. The states use these dollars in various ways, included directly funding initiatives and potentially setting up competitive grant programs.

Table 4.2 shows a short list of the top-ten states ordered by amount of federal funding received as of May 2013. You will see that all of these states individually receive in the billions of dollars. Also, note that there are many transactions taking place to accumulate those sums. It is likely not one big grant program, rather a series of unique transactions and grants being applied for in each state to more than one federal agency.

TABLE 4.2 Top-Ten Federal Grant Funded States

State	Total Dollars	Total Transactions
Virginia	$3.8B	5,790
Massachusetts	$3.6B	16,617
Illinois	$2.1B	2,655
Texas	$1.7B	3,238
California	$1.5B	2,054
Oregon	$1.5B	1,154
Michigan	$1.4B	4,045
New York	$1.4B	3,338
Louisiana	$1.1B	1,898
Tennessee	$1.1B	1,648

Source: "Sub-Award Spending Data," USASpending.gov. Last modified May 8, 2013, usaspending.gov/explore-subaward?fromsubaward=yes.

FOUNDATION AND NONPROFIT GRANTS

Foundations come in many designs structured to meet the financial, tax, and personal wishes of their founders. As such, not every foundation awards grant funding or is a public foundation. Look at some of the common foundation types that follow. *The Only Grant-Writing Book You'll Ever Need*, by Ellen Karsh and Arlen Sue Fox, proved a solid resource for foundation definitions. In their book, the authors define four types of foundations (family, independent private, corporate, and community) that are commonly created to house and subsequently make philanthropic donations or are used as family estate planning vehicles.

Family foundations: A family foundation is primarily used to protect the financial interests of future generations. These are set up and managed by a board of trustees and they work to maintain assets for use at a later time or for distribution in measured doses. Typically, the contributors to such foundations are related, and according to Karsh and Fox they are often managed by family members. Karsh and Fox also indicate that these foundations are not likely to be encountered by grant seekers: "Usually, this type of foundation is quite tight knit and the aims are selective, centering on the special desires of those who founded it."[1]

Independent private foundations: Karsh and Arlen differentiate this structure from the previous one: "Private foundations are ethically, and in most cases, legally bound to follow the donor's intent to the extent possible."[2] As with a family foundation, independent foundations are formed by small groups with defined interests and needs, including families, though not necessarily. They may not be controlled by the original donors (as family foundations are), though, as the authors note, the operations are still expected to reflect the donor's original intent.

Corporate foundations: A corporate foundation is created either by a company, with funds from the company and/or by a company with funds from the founder of the foundation (a large shareholder or company founder is common). Usually, large corporations create these for a variety of business, tax, and social responsibility reasons. The corporate foundation is not tied to the company that sponsored its deployment and they are separate entities.

Community foundations: Community foundations are akin to private and family foundations in that they can include money from a variety or a few donors with a special interest. That interest is typically geared at benefiting a certain place—be it a town or an entire state. Karsh and Fox point out that funds placed into community foundations come from multiple donors and as such these organizations then offer varied grant and other programming to satisfy varied needs of donors. To that end, there could be multiple grants offered with little more programmatic connection than the fact that they all benefit the same community. Awards are

---

1. Ellen Karsh and Arlen Sue Fox, "Foundations," in *The Only Grant-Writing Book You'll Ever Need* (New York: Basic Books, 2009), 16.
2. Ibid.

often smaller than large foundations; however, the funding can still run into the six-figure range for individual projects.

Community and private foundation dollars are typically sourced from individual donors and from funds already placed in trusts by donors or their estates.

After reading through the preceding definitions, you can see that opportunities on a large scale appear to be easier to source by community or corporate foundation. Look at the top community and corporate foundations in Table 4.3, again ordered by giving amount. For much more on foundations, investigate www.foundationcenter.org and search in the funders and funding opportunities sections.

It's clear that these foundations are usually tied to large cities. If you don't live near one of these communities and are not doing a project there, don't despair—search your home region.

TABLE 4.3 Top-Ten Community Foundations by Total Giving

Name/(State)	Total Giving	As of Fiscal Year-End Date
Silicon Valley Community Foundation (CA)	$249,072,000	December 31, 2011
Greater Kansas City Community Foundation (MO)	$218,058,338	December 31, 2011
Foundation for the Carolinas (NC)	$141,521,121	December 31, 2011
The New York Community Trust (NY)	$137,497,141	December 31, 2011
California Community Foundation (CA)	$131,204,000	June 30, 2012
The Columbus Foundation & Affiliated Organizations (OH)	$106,170,746	December 31, 2011
The Chicago Community Trust (IL)	$104,309,814	September 30, 2011
Boston Foundations, Inc. (MA)	$ 98,388,000	June 30, 2012
The San Francisco Foundation (CA)	$ 82,473,000	June 30, 2011
The Cleveland Foundation (OH)	$ 78,670,685	December 31, 2011

Source: "Top Funders," Foundation Center. Last modified May 4, 2013, foundationcenter.org/findfunders/topfunders/top25giving.html.

Corporate Foundations

All of the corporate foundations listed in Table 4.4 are grant makers.

Be certain to check if you see a foundation that interests you—it may not offer competitive grants even though it is a foundation.

The Size of the Philanthropic Marketplace

For nearly 40 years, author Zoltan J. Acs has been fascinated with the connection between entrepreneurship and philanthropy. In his 2013 book, *Why Philanthropy Matters: How the Wealthy Give, and What It Means for Our Economic Well-Being*,[3] Acs, with the support of various other collaborators, examined

> Corporate foundations are independent of the business or company individuals who created them. These funds are from individuals in the company or from the business itself.

TABLE 4.4 Top-Ten Corporate Grant Makers by Total Giving

Name	Total Giving	As of Fiscal Year-End Date
Sanofi Foundation for North America	$497,491,467	December 31, 2011
Novartis Patient Assistance Foundation, Inc.	$331,911,548	December 31, 2011
The Bank of America Charitable Foundation, Inc.	$198,213,418	December 31, 2011
The Wal-Mart Foundation, Inc.	$175,680,474	January 31, 2012
The JPMorgan Chase Foundation	$136,201,550	December 31, 2011
GE Foundation	$112,221,740	December 31, 2010
Wells Fargo Foundation	$107,542,374	December 31, 2011
Citi Foundation	$ 78,614,500	December 31, 2011
The Coca-Cola Foundation, Inc.	$ 76,230,474	December 31, 2011
ExxonMobil Foundation	$ 74,507,597	December 31, 2011

Source: "Top Funders," Foundation Center. Last modified May 4, 2013, foundationcenter.org/findfunders/topfunders/top50giving.html.

---

3. Zoltan J. Acs, *Why Philanthropy Matters: How the Wealthy Give, and What It Means to Our Economic Well-Being* (Princeton: Princeton UP, 2013), 1.

why successful people give. He boils it down to the fact that the philanthropic urge, nay, the moral principle, that many successful individuals have is both a personally held belief and a need to minimize tax liability. Perhaps the giving drive is located somewhere between a desire to live according to the adage "To whom much is given, from them much will be expected" and the business's need to manage tax liability. Acs maintains that the latter is more the aim of very generous entrepreneurs who have made it big.

Take, for example, Acs' discussion of the 2010 Giving Pledge entered into with nearly 40 of America's richest individuals (read billionaires) wherein they planned to give away a full half of their wealth during their lifetimes. He says most press on the Giving Pledge was positive, while some did condemn the would-be donors as grandstanders. Regardless of opinion, the money is momentous. Acs points out the billions of dollars that will go into grants and other programs from these donations and says they add to an already large marketplace (to the tune of $300 billion a year) for contributions to philanthropic causes that already exist.

In Table 4.5, I've included a list from the Foundation Center of the ten largest U.S. foundations categorized by total giving.

Only one, the Bill and Melinda Gates Foundation, tops the billion-dollar amount for annual giving. However, Acs reports that in totaling the assets of the "100 largest foundations in the United States" you'd reach over $232 billion. He goes on to clarify what these assets accomplish in relation to grant funding: "If you look at the hundred largest foundations plus another 1,230 large U.S. foundations, the total amount of grants they make each year is roughly twenty billion dollars."[4] Twenty billion in grants is a major figure.

TRADE ASSOCIATIONS

You are likely a member of one trade organization or another and understand that group's function. Associations can be either for-profit or not-for-profit. They can be organized for member

---

4. Zoltan J. Acs, *Why Philanthropy Matters: How the Wealthy Give, and What It Means to Our Economic Well-Being* (Princeton: Princeton UP, 2013), 111.

TABLE 4.5 Top-Ten U.S. Foundations by Total Giving

Name	Total Giving	As of Fiscal Year-End Date
Bill & Melinda Gates Foundation	$3,239,412,884	December 31, 2011
GlaxoSmithKline Patient Access Programs Foundation	$ 605,399,422	December 31, 2011
Abbott Patient Assistance Foundation	$ 594,182,250	December 31, 2011
Pfizer Patient Assistance Foundation	$ 577,434,110	December 31, 2011
Genentech Access to Care Foundation	$ 553,352,278	December 31, 2011
Lilly Cares Foundation, Inc.	$ 504,948,121	December 31, 2011
Sanofi Foundation for North America	$ 497,491,467	December 31, 2011
Johnson & Johnson Patient Assistance Foundation, Inc.	$ 496,523,981	December 31, 2011
Walton Family Foundation, Inc.	$ 487,795,357	December 31, 2011
Ford Foundation	$ 478,286,000	September 30, 2012

Source: "Top Funders," Foundation Center. Last Modified May 4, 2013, foundationcenter.org/findfunders/topfunders/top100giving.html.

representation politically (i.e., lobbying), or they can be organized to network members across the nation and internationally. Finally, some trade groups exist to provide education and member resources and business tools, including credentialing in specified fields. However, what do trade groups do when it comes to grants?

They do quite a bit. Consider that membership organizations offer grants for obtaining higher education, grants to offset travel for attending conferences, and even very specialized grants that help members, and even former members, with a crisis.

I'm a member of the National Speakers Association (NSA) (www.nsaspeaker.org). Our NSA Foundation acts as a grant-awarding agency as one of its important functions. According to the NSA Foundation 2010–2011 Annual Report, the foundation "distributes up to four percent of the prior year's total assets to annual scholarships, grants, and benevolences."[5]

---

5. "Financials," NSA Foundation 2010–2011 Annual Report, http://www.mynsa.org/portals/0/documents/AnnualReportLowResProof2.pdf (accessed May 3, 2013).

These dollars included two separate grant programs as well as the scholarships offered and the Professional Speakers Benefit Fund, a program that provides financial resources to members, and even former members, with a crisis or those who have outlived their assets.

Trade groups don't look out exclusively for their own members. There are those, including the American Lung Association (ALA), that offer grant funding to support their missions. These awards may or may not be made to members. Look at the programs listed for the ALA in Table 4.6, based on the last review cycle in 2012.

The organization reports that about $273,500 is awarded each year in grants, according to their website and the grants and award listing section.

Trade Associations acquire their grant dollars in various ways, including from member dues, from fees from events, from donations by members, from fundraising drives, and by creating special nonprofit foundations strictly used to provide grant funding for causes deemed important by the membership. Trade associations can win grants from other GFOs and create a grant program with the dollars, thereby offering grant funding as well.

Consider trade organizations that might be interested in your project, mission, or work when you seek grants. Don't forget to explore what funding is available in your own industry groups. Your membership dues just became (even more) worth the money!

Now you're ready for your own Matchmaking 101 between you and the GFOs since you know quite a few of the basics about where grant money originates. For example, you've learned that not all grants are sourced from your tax dollars and not all grants are directed at not-for-profits or academia. Also, one political party is not better or more generous about offering grants than another. All that matters when answering the question, "Is there really any money out there?" is knowing where to look, whether you are a

TABLE 4.6 Grant Funding Statistics for ALA

Grant Type	Applications Received	Number Funded	Percentile Funded To
Lung Health Dissertation Grant	6	1	20.0
Senior Research Training Fellowship	62	11	29.3
Biomedical Research Grant	74	14	20.0
Clinical Patient Care Research Grant	3	1	3.5
Dalsemer Grant	5	1	10.0
Social-Behavioral Research Grant	4	2	16.5
Lung Cancer Discovery Award	30	3	13.3
ALA/AAAAI Allergic Respiratory Disease Award	24	2	14.3

Source: "Past Funding Statistics," American Lung Association, http://www.lung.org/finding-cures/grant-opportunities/grant-offerings.html (accessed May 10, 2013).

fit for the programs you find, and if so, how you get good at acquiring grants.

Dollars abound for those seeking grants; you've seen that in the previous discussion of the funding marketplace. Usually, at this point in my conversation with a prospect, the would-be applicant is at once motivated and overwhelmed with too much information.

PROSPECT: I guess if there is that much money available, somebody is going to win those grants. Might as well be me. But, how do I sort through all of those? Charts with dollar figures are no place to start. Maybe this is just too much to mess with.

CONSULTANT: Don't be discouraged. We've got a plan. You just need to understand which GFO is right for you.

Figure 2.2 (the Grant Funding Path) in Chapter 2 maps the route most commonly taken from idea to grant agreement and ultimately to cash. You can see that everything that starts with the idea and moves to the project. I especially want you to notice the central point in the graphic: the grant agency, or as I've been calling them as a group, *grant funding organizations* (GFOs). GFOs are always the gatekeepers. This fact is critical to your grant funding success; know thy gatekeeper!

> Grant funding organizations (GFOs) are always the gatekeepers.

What Figure 2.2 doesn't demonstrate is how to figure out which GFO (gatekeeper) you should contact. Identifying the right GFO for your project is exceedingly important, and it's often where unsuccessful applicants fail. At this point, you might be wondering if I like to start off applying to every agency that has any possible grant related to your ideas. I know the shotgun approach to grant funding is a bad use of my time and your dollars. I not only discourage it, I simply won't do it.

Say you're planning to visit a friend in an unfamiliar neighborhood. To add to the confusion, you don't know the exact address, but you know the street name, the color and style of the house she owns, and the make of her car, which she says will be parked in front. You've got a little direction, but you're a bit uncertain. Still, it's enough to make the trip—you can figure it out, right? Once you arrive in the general vicinity, would you waste time knocking on the front door of any houses that don't at least match the right color and style or that don't have a car out front? I doubt it; you'd look for the few best choices, perhaps even selecting correctly on the first try. Don't overlook selecting the best-match GFO for your project.

GFOs have money to give. You need money. It sounds like a great plan, and it *can* work. But, just as every date doesn't turn out to be the long-term relationship you seek, the matchmaking part of the GFO-to-project equation can be complex. Still, after reading this chapter, you may be thinking that the objectives of these big-three GFOs overlap. You may still be tempted to apply for everything you see because you've seen the dollar figures. I agree that they overlap, and that's good news because it means options for you. I do have clients that apply for funding through federal sources and foundation sources in the same given year. Your project may fit with multiple GFOs, but time efficiency becomes a problem when you don't select only the best picks and pass on the rest.

Surefire **Misses** *when Targeting GFOs:*
- Applying to all that *seem* to fit
- Applying to any that clearly say they do not fund your type of project
- Applying where you know there is not enough money in the GFO's budget/grant program to merit your time/needs (and assuming that if they receive *your* application, that will change)

Better Aim when Targeting GFOs:
- Research the GFO's previously funded projects for similarities to yours.
- Educate yourself on any political or social slants of the GFO.
- Determine how much funding is available and if it is discretionary or mandated.

PERSPECTIVES ON PROSPERITY

We learned an important lesson during the Great Depression, we learned that lesson again in the recession of the 1990s, and we are learning it again today: America's small businesses will lead our country out of troubled economic times and put us on the path to long-term prosperity prosperity.

—*Karen Mills, 23rd Administrator of the SBA*

The preceding quote was pulled from an op-ed piece posted on the SBA website, entitled "Small Business: The Key to Recovery and Prosperity."[6] Many people, especially entrepreneurs, identify with the ability of small business to make big impact. It has been said that

---

6. Karen Mills, "Small Business: The Key to Recovery and Prosperity," Small Business Administration. Last modified September 1, 2009, http://www.sba.gov/administrator/7390/6117.

if not for small businesses, countries could never rise from financial crisis into prosperity. Small businesses working with grant funding, whether governmental or privately sourced, makes for a potentially complex set of circumstances. Yet, grants given to businesses have an ability to make an impact quickly due to the small business community's trait of quick implementation and streamlined decision making.

I hope this chapter has helped you understand the opportunities that exist in the realm of grant funding. Yes, there really is money, and the locations to look for it are varied and overlap in the scope and mission. As an entrepreneur, you're not used to leaving money on the table. Do grants present an option for you? I think this chapter shows that, due to the sheer size of the market and variety of programs, as well as the number of types of entities that offer grants, it's indeed worth your time to consider grant funding.

At this point, feel free to go through the Project Evaluation Tool in Appendix A with your project in mind. Be sure to revisit it along the way, and then retake it after the conclusion of the book. My intent in offering you this tool is that your readiness improves and that your perspectives on grant funding are realistic and optimistic.

PART TWO

Strategies for Grant Success

CHAPTER FIVE

Finding the Money

> The grant agency isn't exactly begging you to apply and the grant makers don't have you on speed dial.

"What do you mean, you won't take the project?" demanded the man on the other end of the line. It was a prospect I'd known for several months. He called referencing an open funding announcement.

"I'm sorry, Melvin, but you're just not eligible for the funding," I said.

"Of course I am! My company is a perfect fit for this grant! I thought you were a professional at this?" he said, irritated.

I ignored the jab, saying: "That's just it. For-profit companies are not eligible; only municipalities and communities are eligible on this one. You've already said that under no circumstances will you consider partnering. If that is the case, we'll have to pass."

"So, that's just one thing—my not being a nonprofit. Everything else fits! The technology, the timelines—if you won't assist me, I'll find a person who wants my business!" he threatened.

And so he did. A competitor did assist Melvin with the application, but I heard through the grapevine he received a quick response back from the agency:

> We are unable to review your application and it will not be sent on for the national grant competition due to the lack of an eligible applicant.

We've entered Part Two, Grant Strategy, and it's my favorite part of any grant application process. It's also the most important step to securing grant funding. I probably should put a public-advisory label on the cover of this chapter, reading:

> Warning! Do not apply for grants when you are ineligible. Do not
> apply for grants you have no chance to receive!

That's what we are going to discuss in the chapter—your path to funding via the best assessment tools available—your own good sense. This chapter is divided into two parts. First, I discuss tips for finding funding and organizing your funding search efforts and, second, I review how to determine your eligibility and feasibility. Finally, I decode a grant funding announcement and share the sometimes hidden triggers that demonstrate eligibility.

EFFECTIVE SEARCHING

This chapter is about Step 2 of the Prosperity Process: Peruse (Figure 5.1). Using the word *peruse* may make my second step sound leisurely. I know you're not feeling that way when you're hunting for cash, so while I do want you to take time to search the marketplace thoroughly, I believe in efficiency, too. You could hire a consulting firm to find and keep/cull grant opportunities for you, but you might be perfectly suited to scouring for grants yourself. As we go through the chapter, I continue to discuss project and the importance of a correctly identified project as a means to correctly find a grant program fit. Continue to hone the conciseness of your project description as you work through this chapter.

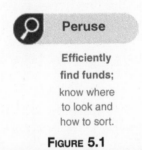

Peruse

Efficiently
find funds;
know where
to look and
how to sort.

FIGURE 5.1

Peruse

Source: Created by Brandrenew.

Funds Follow Fit

To begin the grant searching process, do *not* search for grants.

I bet you're wondering if I mistyped that, but I did not. To best seek grants, quit thinking like a person who wants money and start thinking like a GFO that has a desire to further its mission.

Remember, you're not the one writing the rules, so you must get inside the head of the GFO to make the process work for you. Rather than exclusively looking for available funding, first identify potential target GFOs. Your objective is to learn about what they do, who they are, and the missions they work to promote. Examine all of these pieces with an eye toward ways you could show them potential interest in key aspects of your project. Hunt for information on their home pages, in their annual reports, in lists of previously funded projects, and in their public announcements and marketing. You are seeking to answer the question: "How do I fit?"

> To best seek grants, quit thinking like a person who wants money and start thinking like a GFO that has a desire to further its mission.

Let's say you're inspired to create an environmental education program for youth. Initially, you may think that the EPA (Environmental Protection Agency) would be a great place to apply. Upon looking at their missions and goals, you may see that it appears they are mostly about widespread deployment and tend to make large awards to states and municipalities. Your program, while environmentally themed in one aspect, is really about creating a youth network in your home community. EPA, while they do grants for communities and teachers that are programmatic, is certainly not youth focused. Would I spend time seeking youth programming with this GFO? I would not; I'd peruse resources such as www .foundationcenter.org and use the search engine found there instead. You could also make the judgment not to focus on EPA, in this case, based on the usual applicant types they award. If you are a solopreneur and most awardees appear to be cities and states, it is a good indication that even if you did apply, you would not be eligible, or that you are not in the agency's usual pool of applicants—a factor that could be quite limiting.

Seven Key Questions for Effective Grant Agency Searching

To further pare down the GFO possibilities, next identify the types of projects that the agency tends to fund. Here are some questions to answer that will help determine a solid project-GFO fit:

1. Does the GFO fund construction, implementation, research, programmatic projects, or all of these?

2. Does the agency focus on creating jobs or solving problems and tackling issues?

3. What specific industry sectors and applicant types does the agency tend to award?

4. Is there a clear political bent that the GFO espouses and how does that work for you personally and with your project in mind?

5. Do you have partners/colleagues connected with any of the GFOs you identified?

6. Is your project local, regional, or national in scope, and which of these does the GFO appear to award?

7. Has the GFO recently funded projects similar to yours?

To search efficiently, start not with the grant, but with your project's alignment with the GFO.

Time Efficiency

Everyone *knows* snooping around on social media (aka Facebook stalking and calling it "networking") is just a time waster. Sure, we might still do it, but we know that it's not time efficient. The same is true for spending too much time grant searching online. There are seemingly endless options on large databases like www.grants.gov

or www.fbo.gov and they not only change daily, but change by the minute. You'll never keep up if you simply head to these mega-websites every day and browse. There are many better ways. For starters, if you worked through the seven previous questions, you now know which funders to peruse and what project types those funders like to award. Now, you can use key words and conduct searches with at least two known factors. Now, once you identify an opportunity, it's important to quickly scan for triggers that there is 'live money' available. I have a short list of the top items I always hunt for on my first pass. I recommend locating the following:

- Type of funding announcement or posting
- Close date (when grant is due)
- Open date (when grant is open and accepting applications)
- A list of eligible applicant types
- Amount of funding available
- Maximum dollar award per applicant
- Is the program mandatory or discretionary?

This list appears obvious, but you can be tripped up by some of these, especially the first item on my list. Knowing what type of listing you are looking at is paramount. The agency may list other things besides grant opportunities and they will look similar. You are specifically looking to make certain the GFO uses one of the many phrases or words that indicate the announcement is indeed one listing an available grant.

We will dissect one of these in a later chapter, but first you need to learn that grant funding notices are often disguised by many different names. Here is a partial list of synonyms:

- NOFA—Notice of funds available
- FOA—Funding opportunity announcement
- RFP—Request for proposal
- Open solicitation—the agency is soliciting applications

GRANTS GURU GLOSSARY

Notice of funds available (NOFA), *funding opportunity announcement* (FOA), *request for proposal* (RFP), and *open solicitation* all mean that the grant agency is willing to receive applications and has published guidelines.

For the balance of the book, to keep it simple I'll use just one title: NOFA.

Some grant-listing systems will state whether there are any open funding opportunities, so you can easily figure that out. But, most federal grants listed on www.grants.gov aren't necessarily so direct. You may find a program listed in its entirety, but if the due date is not upcoming, don't assume it's open—it may simply be last year's program archived. Besides not being open right now, this information should not be taken as an invitation for submitting an unsolicited proposal—it isn't. I also like to examine federal grants for mandatory and discretionary funding, particularly if the due date is more than 60 days off or if I am making note of a closed program to check back in the future. Sometimes, you'll see two different amounts, one for the mandatory funding and one for the discretionary. Confirm that the mandatory amount is tied to an open program with a deadline for grant submission. If a program lists only discretionary funding and has no set due date, I would be hesitant to apply based on the assumption that the grant is not assuredly funded. Absolutely confirm the status of the program with the GFO.

Should I Send in Unsolicited Material?

Unsolicited implies any materials, including a complete grant application, submitted to the GFO when no grant notice is apparently available. I do *not* recommend this strategy. For one thing, if you do send something in, don't expect a response. The agency may simply discard materials they did not request. You may receive a polite response or, if you're too persistent, you could incite a negative response from the GFO in the form of a poor first impression. Realize that GFO program managers often work with the same program for years, so they will be the ones reviewing your material. Even if you do not receive the grant or the answer you want, be courteous and follow their basic guidelines so that your next opportunity is not jeopardized. Further, federal grants will have very specific guidelines, so simply sending in a description of your project to an agency contact with no previous introduction is not only unadvisable, it's not worth the time. GFO program managers literally won't have control over funding your project if not funds are allocated at that time to an open solicitation. Wait until you see an open funding announcement.

In the foundation world, unsolicited material may be handled differently. The foundation could offer to accept proposals (that meet their guidelines) at all times. If you see this on the website, keep reading, because that still may not mean you should just send something over. Often, year-round funding cycles imply that you should contact the agency, either through a formal inquiry form or via phone. Once that is done, you will receive direction on whether to submit a proposal. This is more like an invitation, so it's not really unsolicited.

Other Searching Tips

> **Do contact the GFO.** Often, e-mail works best and in some cases it may be the only contact allowed. I've had certain federal agencies where the grant contact listed was exceedingly unhelpful to the point of rudeness. One in particular informed me that if he'd wanted to deal with the public's petty questions, he would have opted for a field job. I've had others, like the USDA example I gave in Part One, that were so helpful it turned my unanswered questions into a career. You will get everything in between; be prepared for it, and not dissuaded by the prospect of dealing with the agency. Most of the time, if you are courteous, concise, and a bit persistent, you'll come away with solid information.

Don't overlook the Q&A section of the announcement. This might offer greater insight into eligibility and feasibility based on past questions from other applicants. Sometimes questions are answered only through a formal process that will have an open and close date. Once responses are all addressed by the GFO, they will post those publically or even e-mail them to interested applicants who have registered to receive updates. Your peers are likely questioning similar aspects of the program as you. Besides getting your questions answered, you are gathering some useful intelligence about the competitive environment for the program.

Even if it were too late to apply this round, if you are interested in the program but are unsure if you fit, I'd take the time and reach out to the GFO. Describe your project, ask questions, and take the occasion to learn about any other possible opportunities on the horizon, or ask to sign up for an e-mail blast with news. I also ask if the contact knows of related funding administered by other program managers in that office. This strategy almost always yields me another contact, an e-mail introduction, or even a direct phone transfer right away. Keep digging everywhere you look and when you have a live one on the line—hold on.

Join groups in your industry online, including those specific to funding, grants, and your trade. Sites like LinkedIn have such groups and I myself post grant openings in groups where I am active and the members are potentially interested. As you know, I follow the agricultural, environmental, and energy sectors. I'm a member of numerous trade groups and online groups and receive their newsletters. These often list funding announcements. To manage the inbox influx, create a separate e-mail account for these newsletters and check it once a week. Once you find a program of interest, start the conversation with the GFO, as noted earlier.

Another great way to become a better browser is by learning more about the industry and the GFOs. Grant makers are hosting webinars, conference calls, and even roundtable events at an increasing rate. This is a wonderful resource for grant seekers. Some of them are purely informational while others will walk you through a grant application template and provide tips for specific applications. This is invaluable education straight from the source.

Always make every connection possible to stay informed. I offer a free newsletter with grant funding opportunities each month. Most agencies will do the same. Collect a variety of these contacts for the timeliest information and access and you'll spend very little time lost in the big databases without direction.

Create a Grant Tracking System

Once you begin to find solid funding leads, manage your searches and opportunities diligently. Why rework when you can create a follow-up system early in the process. I should warn you that if you don't create something, you'll just misplace your search results eventually. It's fine to maintain more than just a folder, even an online folder or e-mail folder/file, but if you're like me, you'll never check that proverbial dumping ground. Take the time to create a better-quality system, such as my personal grant calendar, to house the funding opportunities you are following. Once you've built a database, don't overlook a system for alerts that you *will* heed, or those neatly categorized opportunities will pass you by.

There are a couple of points to make about the grant calendar (Table 5.1). The first is duration. Grant funding is a long cycle, so don't search for opportunities only in the next few months. Seek those that are interesting but may not open for as much as a year from now. The agency may never have that program again or they may open it sooner; you don't know this if you're not monitoring it. The other reason for a long timeframe involves what is required. You may find an open funding announcement only to see that you need a feasibility study or that you must have conducted a member survey with a certain number of responses to be eligible. If you haven't done this work, don't apply; rather decide if this funding opportunity would be worth the pre-work and begin that process now.

TABLE 5.1 Funding Opportunities Calendar

Date	Agency	Program	Action
1/15/13	NSF	Energy for Sustainability	Grant Opening
1/15/13	NSF	Environmental Engineering	Grant Opening
1/30/13	USDA	Rural Energy for America Program	TBD Grant Opening
2/1/13	EPA	Clean Diesel Emerging Technologies	TBD Proposal Due
2/10/13	OCRA CDBG	Community Focus Funds	TBD Proposal Due
2/11/13	DOE EERE	Advancements in Algal Biomass Yield	Concept Paper Due
2/19/13	NSF	Energy for Sustainability	Proposal Due
2/19/13	NSF	Environmental Engineering	Proposal Due
3/1/13	USDA	Conservation Innovation Grants	TBD Grant Opening
3/30/13	USDA	REAP Grant Only	TBD Proposal Due
3/30/13	OCRA CDBG	Main Street Revitalization	TBD Proposal Due
4/1/13	DOE EERE	Advancements in Algal Biomass	Proposal Due
4/14/13	USDA	Conservation Innovation Grants	TBD Proposal Due
4/20/13	OCRA CDBG	Community Focus Funds	TBD Application Due
4/24/13	USDA DOE	Biomass Research & Development Initiative	TBD Pre-Proposal Due
4/26/13	KADF	Renewable Energy Initiative	Application Due
5/1/13	DHS	Science & Technology SBIR	TBD Phase I App Due
5/22/13	AFRI	—Rural Families, Comm. & Regional Development	Application Due
5/22/13	AFRI	—Economics, Markets and Trade	Application Due
5/22/13	AFRI	—Environment	Application Due
6/8/13	OCRA CDBG	Main Street Revitalization	TBD Application Due
6/11/13	IDEM	Recycling Market Development Program	TBD Proposal Due

Date	Agency	Program	Status
6/13/13	USDA DOE	Biomass Research & Development Initiative	TBD Grant Opening
6/14/13	USDA	SBIR	TBD Grant Opening
6/29/13	USDA	REAP Guaranteed Loan Only	TBD Proposal Due
8/3/13	USDA DOE	Biomass Research & Development Initiative	TBD Proposal Due
9/13/13	USDA	SBIR	TBD Proposal Due
10/1/13	USDA	Solid Waste Management Grant	Grant Opening
11/1/13	DHS	Science & Technology SBIR	TBD Phase I App Due
11/20/13	AFRI	RFA—Engineering, Products & Processes	TBD LOI Due
12/3/13	NSF	SBIR Phase I	TBD Proposal Due
12/17/13	DOE	SBIR & STTR	TBD LOI Due
12/18/13	DOE/USDA	Plant Feedstock Genomics for Bioenergy	TBD Pre-proposal Due
12/31/13	USDA	Solid Waste Management Grant	Proposal Due
12/31/13	AFRI	Climate Variability & Change Challenge	TBD LOI Due
1/28/14	AFRI	Sustainable Bioenergy Area	TBD LOI Due
2/13/14	AFRI	RFA—Engineering, Products & Processes	TBD Application Due
2/25/14	DOE/USDA	Plant Feedstock Genomics for Bioenergy	TBD Application Due

I like to further break down the grants I'm monitoring by month. That way, if I know a program usually opens/closes in a given month, I will search a few months before and a few months after when I'm ready to look for it. I also use the TBD (to be determined) acronym to indicate that the program opened or closed on that date last year and I want to check again this year around that timeframe. Finally, you'll see that in the action column we have separate entries for open and close dates as well as entries for additional actions besides a grant application, like the due date for a concept paper. If there is a required action with a due date tied to it from the GFO, then that is a required date for your application, too.

DETERMINING ELIGIBILITY AND FEASIBILITY (STEP 3)

This is the "is-the-risk-worth-it?" junction for each grant application process and I take it very seriously. As an applicant, you should, too.

There are two key questions to ask once you've found a decent grant funding opportunity:

1. Am I technically eligible?
2. Is it feasible that I will win an award?

Critically evaluating these factors can be confusing. I have a few pointers. First, eligibility must be locked down tight—either you are eligible, or you are not. Feasibility determination is more nebulous and tied to your acceptance of risk for reward. Caution to entrepreneurs: Don't automatically say "I'm an entrepreneur; I have a higher tolerance for risk than most!" That really doesn't apply here. Because we are so limited in the ability to control the outcome of the grant, I prefer to take control of the outcome at the outset. I never guarantee an applicant funding—it is impossible. I've seen applications I didn't love receive funding and those I thought were near-perfect lose out. I can never be 100 percent certain. However, my motto is "Be 90 percent sure." That means, be 90 percent sure you can win and most of the time you will.

I should add that other grant preparers might not agree. Applicants often feel this 90 percent rule is an extremely conservative benchmark in the decision whether to apply. That's okay with me, because I know what has worked in my experience. I also know that when prospects tell me they have a high tolerance for risk, they mean it, but if they don't necessarily understand grant funding, they may not realize how little control they have. Besides, my client base expects results, and while there is a high tolerance for risk, there is an equally higher expectation of performance. Entrepreneurs don't accept failure well since they usually have a high standard for excellence. I do not like unhappy clients, so I use my 90 percent rule.

Good news about grant funding: I know that entrepreneurs are experts at risk assessment and I think this section will come easy now that you have a few no-fail tips to determine whether you fit.

The third step in my process has caused many a client of mine to yawn. "Why ponder? Let's go!" is a common refrain. That's exactly what I'm doing. I am moving forward in the decision-making process by helping to ensure a greater likelihood of success. *Ponder* does imply taking time to think through something and that is exactly what I'm asking you to do here.

Eligibility Assessment

Eligibility is something we cannot affect much at the time of grant application. We may be able to do that during a comment period following the grant review period or through things like meeting with the GFO and lobbying, but once the notice is published, eligibility is pretty firm. We start by reviewing a notice that funds are available.

As you will see in the grant announcement that concludes this chapter, there are clues that help you determine eligibility. Eligibility is in no way standardized across grants, agencies, or even within a given program year to year. GFOs will create many of their own very unique eligibility criteria, so look carefully. However, there are certain criteria that are consistent. Here's a checklist of items I recommend seeking for each grant. At a minimum, determine your eligibility every time for the following seven items:

Basic Eligibility Checklist:
1. **Applicant type:** This is your business entity status, such as for-profit, nonprofit, individual, academic, municipality, and so on. Applicant type may also include a citizenship clause—whether the program is interested in helping mostly U.S. citizens or the goal is to award grants that benefit other countries are both possibilities.

2. **Project type:** This is your project description and in part the scope of work your project entails. This can be the most difficult to determine because there may be several criteria to fit.

3. **Location of performance:** This may mean the site of the project or it could simply mean the region of the country or world. It may also mean where contracts originate or what geographical locations your project will benefit.

4. **Purpose:** Your project must serve the same goals as the agency wishes to promote. Read this to determine your alignment with the GFO.

5. **Timeline:** Eligibility should be determined for both project start and end dates and when all funds must be used.

6. **Use of funds:** Funders will tell you what you can and cannot buy with their dollars. Heed this carefully. If what you need to buy is not eligible (say you want equipment and only design and engineering are eligible), you are not likely a fit.

7. **Certifications:** The agency will require that you attest via signature or possibly provide proof for a variety of certifications. For example, you may have to certify that you've not been convicted of a felony or that the company applying has not been bankrupt in the last two years.

As a last word on eligibility, recall the story of Melvin—as an applicant, he was not eligible, even though the rest of the project fit well. If you cannot meet all eligibility criteria, you are not partially eligible, you are ineligible.

Feasibility Assessment

A while ago, a prospect called as he had received my free newsletter from an existing client of mine. In the newsletter, I listed an open grant with a $500,000 maximum award. The client who forwarded this actually won this grant several years earlier and sent it over to a colleague looking to do a similar energy project. I learned about his project and goals and we talked for a while. When my client applied, there was more than $40 million available in the initiative; last year's program noted $3.5 million available and part of that for loan guarantees, not grants. The pot was much smaller. I explained that asking for nearly 15 percent of the overall pie would be challenging to score—even though the notice indicated that the maximum grant request was still set at $500,000, as before. I went on to point out that while the technology he wanted to implement was still listed as eligible, I'd not seen any others awarded for this in two years. I also told him there were now priority points for other technologies, meaning his application would automatically score a little lower. In a competitive program, I didn't think he could win an award. Finally, the agency head had been under fire in recent months for awarding applications using this same kind of technology that failed. The bad press didn't entice me into applying because I believed these projects were quite cold at the reviewer's level. I recommended the applicant not apply.

This is a common situation: The applicant is eligible, but the likelihood of winning is lower than the client (or my) threshold for the potential pain of not winning. In the previous example, the prospect had the benefit of my experience to advise him against applying. However, if you're going this alone, how do you determine feasibility?

Clues for Assessing Award Feasibility:
- What has the grant agency funded in the past?
- How would your project compare to previously funded projects?

- Is the trend for your kind of project steady, increasing, or decreasing in terms of number of award winners?
- How many grants have been funded in the past?
- How much money is in the program compared to what you are asking for? Are you asking for a reasonable amount within the scope of this program's allotment?
- Is the amount of funding and the size of awards trending up, down, or staying the same?
- What is the average size of past awards?
- Are there preferences or extra points for certain kinds of grant requests?
- Could your project fit in a preferential category, if any are listed?

Outside of just not applying, are there other alternatives if the project is eligible but doesn't look feasible?

- Ask for less funding.
- Remove portions of the project to improve the scope more toward what the agency wants to fund or limit the portions less desirable—even if you want to complete those with other funding.
- Consider partnerships, if applicant type is an area where you don't fit.
- Ask staff at the agency what they think. They might not tell you whether you should apply; it's true your GFO program manager is not in the business of advising. However, you might be surprised, so I would inquire when in doubt. Even if they won't offer a firm answer, perhaps they'll provide some insight with figures about past awards or other information that implies what they do and do not fund.

Grant funding success is all about thinking strategically.

Grant funding success is all about thinking strategically.

How would you evaluate this decision for your business if it weren't an opportunity for "free money"? Does that make a difference?

I have seen the notion of winning a grant alter the ego of ordinarily savvy businesspeople. Apparently this carrot of cash makes some people invent angles and ideas, which are really just hopes they are pinning to a kite, or messages placed in a bottle—they wouldn't ordinarily see the decision that way, but they just can't help it! Don't let this grant brain-drain happen to you. I am all for creativity—that's one of my reasons for authoring this book—but not at the expense of sound judgment.

DECODING FEDERAL GRANT ANNOUNCEMENTS

It's time to crack the code words and phrases common to finding funding. I started teaching this section in my grant training classes two years ago, once I realized that finding the grant notice, while obviously essential, is only half of the job. Once they get it open and see the lingo, the possible redundancy, the litany of terminology, and just the sheer volume of pages to review, I know some would-be applicants just give up. Don't do that! Instead, read on and learn how to weed through the funding announcement carefully; you just need a little time and an eye for detail.

Figure 5.2 shows the actual front page of a grant announcement for the USDA's Value Added Producer Grant program. It's just a snapshot meant to show you what the grant announcement will commonly look like as seen in the daily *Federal Register*. Because the announcement is quite long and in this case very industry specific, I chose to adapt it in what follows so that I could go through and highlight key concepts, leaving out excessive details that would confuse. I selected an industry-specific grant to illustrate how tightly niched grant funding announcements and grants in general are.

Another feature here is that this grant includes several subcategories. The same applicant will not fit into each category offered, so it is incumbent on would-be applicants to carefully select their best fit by both eligibility and feasibility. Eligibility is first. Then, in the case of a program like this one, the applicant may be eligible for

FINDING THE MONEY

ADDRESSES: The meeting will be held at the Alpine Early Learning Center, 100 Foothill Road, Markleeville, CA.

Written comments may be submitted as described under Supplementary Information. All comments, including names and addresses when provided, are placed in the record and are available for public inspection and copying. The public may inspect comments received at the Carson Ranger District, 1536 S. Carson St, Carson City, NV. Please call ahead to 775–884–8140 to facilitate entry into the building to view comments.

FOR FURTHER INFORMATION CONTACT: Daniel Morris, RAC Coordinator, Carson Ranger District, 775–884–8140, *danielmorris@fs.fed.us.*

Individuals who use telecommunication devices for the deaf (TDD) may call the Federal Information Relay Service (FIRS) at 1–800–877–8339 between 8 a.m. and 8 p.m., Eastern Standard Time, Monday through Friday.

SUPPLEMENTARY INFORMATION: The following business will be conducted: (1) Review and recommend funding allocation for proposed projects for 2012 funding (2) Public Comment. Anyone who would like to bring related matters to the attention of the committee may file written statements with the committee staff before or after the meeting. Written comments and requests for time for oral comments must be sent to 1536 S. Carson St., Carson City, NV. 89701, or by email to *danielmorris@fs.fed.us*, or via facsimile to 775–884–8199. A summary of the meeting will be posted at *https:// fsplaces.fs.fed.us/fsfiles/unit/wo/ secure_rural_schools.nsf* within 21 days of the meeting.

Meeting Accommodations: If you require sign language interpreting, assistive listening devices or other reasonable accommodation for access to the meeting please request this in advance by contacting the person listed in the section titled **FOR FURTHER INFORMATION CONTACT.** All reasonable accommodation requests are managed on a case by case basis.

Dated: August 9, 2012.

David M. Palmer,
Acting District Ranger.
[FR Doc. 2012–20015 Filed 8–14–12; 8:45 am]
BILLING CODE 3410-11-P

DEPARTMENT OF AGRICULTURE

Rural Business-Cooperative Service

Inviting Applications for Value-Added Producer Grants

AGENCY: Rural Business-Cooperative Service, USDA.

ACTION: Notice of Funding Availability (NOFA).

SUMMARY: USDA announces the availability of grants through the Value-Added Producer Grant (VAPG) program for Fiscal Year 2012. Approximately $14 million in competitive grant funds for FY 2012 is available to help agricultural producers enter into value-added activities. At the discretion of the Secretary, additional funds may be made available to qualified ranking applications that respond to this announcement from prior year carry-over funds.

Awards may be made for either economic planning or working capital activities related to the processing and/or marketing of valued-added agricultural products. The maximum grant amount for a planning grant is $100,000 and the maximum grant amount for a working capital grant is $300,000.

There is a matching funds requirement of at least $1 for every $1 in grant funds provided by the Agency (matching funds plus grant funds must equal proposed total project costs). Matching funds may be in the form of cash or eligible in-kind contributions and may be used only for eligible project purposes. Matching funds must be available at time of application and must be certified and verified as described in 7 CFR 4284.931(b)(3) and (4). See 7 CFR 4284.923 and 7 CFR 4284.924 for examples of eligible and ineligible uses of matching funds.

Ten percent of available funds are reserved to fund applications submitted by Beginning Farmers or Ranchers and Socially Disadvantaged Farmers or Ranchers, and an additional 10 percent of available funds are reserved to fund applications from farmers or ranchers that propose development of Mid-Tier Value Chain projects (both collectively referred to as "reserved funds"). See 7 CFR 4284.925 and 7 U.S.C. 1632(a).

DATES: You must submit your application by October 15, 2012 or it will not be considered for funding announced in this Notice. Paper applications must be postmarked and mailed, shipped or sent overnight by this date. Electronic applications are permitted via www.grants.gov only, and

must be received before midnight on this date.

ADDRESSES: You should contact your USDA Rural Development State Office if you have questions about eligibility or submission requirements. You are encouraged to contact your State Office well in advance of the application deadline to discuss your project and to ask any questions about the application process. You may request technical assistance from your State Office up to 14 days prior to the application deadline. Application materials are available at *http:// www.rurdev.usda.gov/BCP_VAPG.html.*

If you want to submit an electronic application, follow the instructions for the VAPG funding announcement on *http://www.grants.gov.* If you want to submit a paper application, send it to the State Office located in the State where your project will primarily take place. You can find State Office Contact information at *http:// www.rurdev.usda.gov/recd_map.html* or see the following list:

Alabama
USDA Rural Development State Office, Sterling Centre, Suite 601, 4121 Carmichael Road, Montgomery, AL 36106–3683, (334) 279–3400/TDD (334) 279–3495.

Alaska
USDA Rural Development State Office, 800 West Evergreen, Suite 201, Palmer, AK 99645–6539, (907) 761–7705/TDD (907) 761–8905.

American Samoa (see Hawaii)

Arizona
USDA Rural Development State Office, 230 N. 1st Ave., Suite 206, Phoenix, AZ 85003, (602) 280–8701/TDD (602) 280–8705.

Arkansas
USDA Rural Development State Office, 700 West Capitol Avenue, Room 3416, Little Rock, AR 72201–3225, (501) 301–3200/ TDD (501) 301–3279.

California
USDA Rural Development State Office, 430 G Street, # 4169, Davis, CA 95616–4169, (530) 792–5800/TDD (530) 792–5848.

Colorado
USDA Rural Development State Office, Denver Federal Center, Building 56, Room 2300, PO Box 25426, Denver, CO 80225–0426, (720) 544–2903.

Commonwealth of the Northern Marianas Islands-CNMI (see Hawaii)

Connecticut (see Massachusetts)

Delaware-Maryland
USDA Rural Development State Office, 1221 College Park Drive, Suite 200, Dover, DE 19904, (302) 857–3580/TDD (302) 857–3585.

FIGURE 5.2

Front Page of USDA Value-Added Producer Grant Notice of Funding Availability from 2012 as Seen in the *Federal Register*

Source: Federal Register, Vol. 77 (August 15, 2012).

more than one area (or fit only in one area). If that is the case, feasibility for success should be critically assessed and weighed.

For the adapted grant announcement that follows, the GFO's information appears first, and my guidance follows each item in italicized text.

> Department of Agriculture
> Value-Added Producer Grants
> Agency:
> Rural Business Cooperative Service, USDA

The agency name, USDA or Department of Agriculture, may be followed by a subdivision, in this case, the Rural Business Cooperative Service. This is important as the needs of differing subdivisions will vary as will their focus and programs.

> Action:
> Notice of Funding Availability (NOFA)

Always check the action section to ensure that you are reading a current grant announcement and not another document that is published in the Federal Register *such as a notice of comment period.*

> Executive Summary:
> USDA Announces the availability of grants through the Value-Added Producer Grant (VAPG) program for Fiscal Year 2012. Approximately $14 million in competitive grant funds for FY 2012 is available to help agricultural producers enter into value-added activities. At the discretion of the Secretary, additional funds may be made available to qualified ranking applications that respond to this announcement from prior year carry-over funds.
>
> Awards may be made for either economic planning or working capital activities related to the processing and/or marketing of value-added agricultural products. The maximum grant amount for a planning grant is $100,000 and the maximum grant amount for a working capital grant is $300,000.
>
> There is a matching funds requirement of at least $1 for every $1 in grant funds provided by the Agency (matching funds plus grant funds must equal proposed total project costs). Matching funds may be in the form of cash or eligible in-kind contributions and may be used only for

eligible project purposes. Matching funds must be available at time of application and described in 7 CFFR 4284.931(b)(3) and (4). See 7 CFR 4284.923 and 7 CFR 4284.924 for examples of eligible and ineligible uses of matching funds.

Ten percent of available funds are reserved to fund applications submitted by beginning Farmers or Ranchers and Socially Disadvantaged Farmers or Ranchers, and an additional 10 percent of available funds are reserved to fund applications from farmers or ranchers that propose development of Mid-Tier Value Chain projects (both collectively referred to as "reserved funds").

The summary is just that, a summary. Obviously, it's a great place to start and gage an initial eligibility. However, as you'll see, not everything important is listed here, including the multiple tiers of eligibility requirements with this program. Do not base your final decision to apply for a grant on an executive summary of the program.

Dates:
You must submit your application by October 15, 2012 or it will not be considered for funding announced in this Notice. Paper applications must be postmarked and mailed, shipped, or sent overnight by this date. Electronic applications are permitted via www. grants.gov only and must be received before midnight on this date.

Obviously, you need to know the due date for the application, but you should also look for a time of day it is due and if that is due by that time in a certain time zone or in your own local time zone (the deadline can be that specific). Whatever the deadline time is, it's not negotiable. This section will also tell you about the submission options. You can see that this grant could be mailed or sent through an online system. Submit via only one of the listed options.

Funding Opportunity Description:
Purpose of the Program
The primary objective of this grant program is to help Independent Producer of agricultural commodities, Agriculture Producer Groups, Farmer and Rancher Cooperatives, and Majority-Controlled Producer-Based Business Ventures enter into value-added activities related to the processing and/or marketing of bio-based value-added agricultural products. Grants will be awarded competitively for

DECODING FEDERAL GRANT ANNOUNCEMENTS

either planning or working capital projects directly related to the processing and/or marketing of value-added products. Generating new products, creating and expanding marketing opportunities, and increasing producer income are the end goals. Applications that support aspects of regional strategic planning, cooperative development, sustainable farming, and local and regional food systems are encouraged. Proposals must demonstrate economic viability and sustainability in order to compete for funding.

This section further describes the program, may provide some background on the funding opportunity's purpose, and will explain why the program exists. This is very important—more so than you may think at first glance. Always return back to the purpose somewhere in your narrative.

Award Information:

Fiscal Year Funds: FY 2012
   Approximate Number of Awards: 120.
   Available Total Funding: Approximately $14 million.
   Minimum Award Amount: Not restricted for planning or working capital. In FY 2011, 49 percent of awards were $50,000 or less.
   Maximum Award Amount: Planning—$100,000; Working Capital—$300,000
Anticipated Award Date: January 18, 2013.
   Grant Period Length: The Maximum grant period is 3 years from the date of award. Proposed grant periods should be scaled to the complexity of the objectives of the project.

Of course, applicants are very interested in this section, which provides the cash details and when it should be available. A couple of highlights here include the minimum or maximum award levels. Be sure to correctly calculate your grant request based on the percentage of match required and the maximum or minimum award allowed. This program does not have a minimum, but many do. I once had a prospect call me because she had applied for a grant that was turned down due to her not having requested enough money.

A little secret in here is the line that says "proposed grant periods should be scaled to the complexity of the objectives of the project." What this tells me is that you don't want to ask for the maximum grant for a large, detailed project and then ask them to fund it in one year when similar work might take two or three (and there are allowances for that in this grant). Applicants will often want to do this in order to get the funding up front and quickly, but that strategy could backfire. If your project can conceivably be completed in a short time, that is fine as long as you convincingly make that case

Eligibility Information:
Eligible Applicants
You must be an Independent Producer Group, Farmer or Rancher Cooperative, or a Majority Controlled Producer-Based Business to apply to this program; and you must meet all related requirements for Emerging Market (as applicable), Citizenship, Legal Authority and Responsibility, Multiple Grants and Active Grants. In addition, you must meet Departmental requirements related to debarment, suspension and exclusions from participation in Federal assistance programs, as well as requirements related to outstanding Federal income taxes, judgments and delinquencies. For detailed requirements, see 7 CFR 4283.920 and 7 CFR 4284.921.

Here is the first pass on eligibility for this grant, which includes both applicant and project eligibility terms. Read them carefully; they cover several possible options and in this case they are very industry specific.

As a special emphasis, Rural Development encourages applications from Federally Recognized Tribal Groups and corporations and subdivisions of Tribal Groups undertaking or planning to undertake eligible value-added projects. For further tribal eligibility questions, please contact your local Rural Development Office.

If you see a special emphasis, look later in the document for any points or merit criteria that may be associated with this. They may also reserve a certain amount of dollars for the special-emphasis group.

Project Eligibility
Your project must meet (1) Product Eligibility requirement related to the definition of Value-Added Agricultural Product, including value-added methodologies, expansion of customer base for the agricultural commodity, and increased revenues returning to the

applicant's producers of the agricultural commodity as a result of the project; (2) Purpose Eligibility requirement related to the maximum grant amounts, certification and verification of matching funds for planning or working capital activities, including requirements related to the conflicts of interest and ineligible expenses in excess of 10 percent of total project costs, a substantive work plan and budget, independent feasibility study and/or business plan

The possible types of projects are detailed in this section and are tightly delineated. If I were unsure whether my project met the criteria, I would make a call to the GFO for clarification

Other Eligibility Requirements
Grant Period Eligibility
Your project timeframe or grant period can be a maximum of 36 months in length from the date of award. Your proposed grant period should begin no earlier than the anticipated award announcement date herein, January 18, 2013, and should end no later than 36 months following that date. Your project activities must begin within 90 days of that date of award. If you request funds for a time period beginning before January 18, 2013, and/or ending later than 36 months from the date, your applications will be ineligible.
Ineligible Expenses
Applications with ineligible expenses of more than 10 percent of total project costs will be ineligible to compete for funds. Eligible applications that are selected for award but contain ineligible expenses of 10 percent or less of total project costs must remove those ineligible expenses from the final project budget that is subject to approval by the Agency. See 7 CFR 4284.923 for examples of eligible planning and working capital use of funds, and see 7 CFR 4284.924 for examples of ineligible use of funds.

This section includes yet a third eligibility determination after applicant and project—and that is grant period. Very important to note is that the project cannot begin until after the grant award is made and they offer the possible date (yes, I said possible *date; you should not assume that is guaranteed!) of award. Decide if you can delay beginning your work until this time before applying.*

I also like how this program is clear about ineligible expenses—double-check that your budget doesn't include them.

> Reserved Funds:
> In response to this announcement, 10 percent of total funding available will be used to fund projects that benefit Beginning Farmer or Ranchers, or Socially-Disadvantaged Farmers or Ranchers. In Addition, 10 percent of total funding available will be used to fund projects that propose development of Mid-Tier Value Chains as part of a Local or Regional Supply Chain Network. See related definitions in 7 CFR 4284.902.

As I mentioned earlier, this grant gave away the information that funds would be set aside or reserved for certain individuals or groups. The percentage of funds is even listed. You should take a look at this and determine how the 20 percent of the possible funding pool noted here affects your application. If you don't fit into one of these reserved categories, it doesn't mean you should avoid applying, but it does mean you are now competing for a 20 percent smaller pool of dollars. That's another reason I advocate scoring your application as a grant feasibility strategy. Also, don't assume you fit into the reserve funding until you check the regulation mentioned for the exact detail (the 7 CFR is the regulation and it can be easily found with a Google search). The GFO will have clear rules for who and what qualifies for these special categories.

> Application Scoring:
> The agency will only score applications in which the applicant and project are eligible, which are complete and sufficiently responsive to program requirements, and in which the Agency agrees on the likelihood of financial feasibility for working capital requests.

The previous statement means that you won't even be scored or get any farther than the door if you don't submit a complete, eligible application. This perfectly illustrates why I never advocate turning in applications where you might fit. It's a waste of time.

> We will score your application according to the procedures and criteria specified in 7 CFR 4284.942, and with tiered scoring thresholds as specified below.

For each criterion, you must show how the project has merit and why it is likely to be successful. If you do not address all parts of the criterion, or do not sufficiently communicate relevant project information, you will receive lower scores. The maximum number of points that can be awarded to your application is 100. For this announcement, there is no minimum score requirement for funding. Note: If you are submitting a working capital application that requires a feasibility study and/or business plan, you must submit those documents along with your application. In addition, you must summarize within your application relevant results of the feasibility study/business plan in response to the scoring criteria, as applicable, because reviewers will not receive copies of your feasibility study/business plan when evaluating your proposal and assigning scores. The Agency application package provides additional instruction to help you to respond to the criteria below.

The GFO is very exacting in what they will and won't tolerate on this grant as it relates to score. They even provide a maximum score, which is a great tool for determining feasibility once you go through the scoring criteria and assess yourself.

I will not go through a detailed explanation of each of the scoring criteria below, though should you be responding to this grant announcement, you would want to read each carefully and tabulate a score for each criterion. You can see on first glance, however, that for each one, there is a possible score of 0 to 30 points,. That means the score is subjective. Even a zero score is subjective. However, as long as you submitted something for each category, it is unlikely you would receive no points,

1. Nature of the Proposed Venture
   (Graduated Score 0–30 Points)
   For both planning and working capital grants, you should discuss the technical feasibility of the project, as well as the operations efficiency, profitability, and overall economic sustainability resulting from the project. In addition, demonstrate the potential for expanding the customer base for the agricultural commodity or value-added product, and the expected increase in revenue returns to the producer-owners providing the majority of the raw agricultural commodity to the project.

Points will be awarded as follows:

- 0 points will be awarded if you do not substantively address this criterion

- 10 points will be awarded if the criterion is poorly addressed

- 20 points will be awarded if the criterion is partially addressed

- 30 points will be awarded if you clearly articulate the rationale for the project and show a high likelihood of success based on technological feasibility and economic sustainability.

2. Qualifications of Project Personnel
   (Graduated Score 0–20 Points)
   You should identify and describe the qualifications of each person responsible for leading or managing the total project, as well as the people responsible for actually conducting the individual tasks in the work plan. You should discuss the credentials, education, capabilities, experience, availability and commitment of each person working on the project. If staff or consultants have not been selected at the time of application, you should describe the qualifications required for the positions to be filled.Points will be awarded as follows:

   - 0 points will be awarded if you do not substantively address this criterion

   - 10 points will be awarded if at least one of the identified staff or consultants demonstrates 5 or more years of relevant experience; or, if no project personnel have been identified but necessary qualifications for the positions to be filled are clearly described.

   - 20 points will be awarded if all of the identified staff demonstrates relevant qualifications and experience.

3. Commitments and Support
   (Graduated Score of 0–10 Points)
   Your application must show that the project has a strong direct financial, technical and logistical support from agricultural producers, end-users, and other third party contributors who are necessary for the successful completion of the project. All cash or in-kind contributions from producers, end users, or other contributors should be discussed. End-user commitments may include contracts or letters of intent or interest in purchasing the value-added product. Third-party commitments may include evidence of critical

partnerships, logistical, or technical support necessary for the project to succeed.

Points will be awarded as follows:

- 0 points will be awarded if you do not show that you have quality commitments or support from producers, end-users or other critical third party contributors.

- 5 points will be awarded if you partially show real, high quality direct support or commitments from at least one producer, end user, or other third party contributor.

- 10 points will be awarded if you show real, high quality direct support or commitments from multiple producers, end-users and critical third-party contributors.

4. Work Plan and Budget
(Graduated Score of 0–20 Points)
You must submit a comprehensive work plan and budget (for full details, see 7 CFR 4284.922(b)(5)). Your work plan must provide specific and detailed descriptions of the tasks and the key project personnel that will accomplish the projects goals. The budget must present a detailed breakdown of all estimated costs of project activities and allocate those costs among the listed tasks. You must show the source and use of both grant and matching funds for all tasks. Matching funds must be spent at a rate equal to, or in advance of, grant funds and eligible start and end date for the project and for individual project tasks must be clearly shown and may not exceed Agency specified timeframes for the grant period. Working Capital applications must include an estimate of Program Income expected to be earned during the grant period (see 7 CFR 3019.24).

- 0 points will be awarded if the work plan and budget do not substantively address this criterion.

- 10 points will be awarded if the work plan and budget only partially address this criterion

- 20 points will be awarded if a detailed, comprehensive work plan and budget is provided.

It is not uncommon for GFOs to list their scoring criteria as well as the points assigned to each score in the FOA. I like it when this is available. If you have this information, use it. Score your application! I cover how to create a viable self-score in Chapter 10. It would be a good idea to learn more scoring process and then create a practice score using this as an example.

PERSPECTIVES ON PROSPERITY

> All prosperity begins in the mind and is dependent only upon the full
> use of our creative imagination.
> —*Ruth Ross, psychologist and author of* Prosperity Principles

Clients ask me if I see myself as a technical writer or perhaps a project manager. Some ask me if I have a degree in finance or an MBA. None of these applies. I have an agricultural communications degree and am essentially a writer/speaker. When I think of myself, though, I simply believe I'm a creative type. Though I often work with highly industrial projects and more professional engineers than professional artists, I'm not the technical engineering type. My role is to bring a creative bent to the project while still coloring inside the lines.

The key learning here concerns strategy. Always work through the following when evaluating a funding decision. First is eligibility; second is feasibility.

As you evaluate grant funding for your businesses ventures and personal projects, I encourage you to harness both creativity and a knack for understanding the hand you are dealt. I know I cannot change the guidelines and I cannot be the grant reviewer, so I look for ways I can affect the project long before the application is complete. For these reasons, I believe grant funding, with all of its regulations in tow, is still an interesting fit for entrepreneurs. You know how to find alternatives when looking at what everyone else sees as the same. You understand innovation in a land of conformity. You'll figure out grant funding, too.

CHAPTER SIX

Is There a Grant for That?

> You've just realized the grant funding world is wide open with opportunity, but your idea is a long way from a project. You need a little help getting started.

Larissa, a friend of mine active in local politics, had previously been in county government and done grant writing for community projects. Our conversations often turned to funding—mostly problems with it and being without it. A couple of years back, we were out to lunch when, toward the end of the meal, she looked a little sheepish and said:

"I hate to ask, because it's probably nothing and I hate to admit it's probably a waste of your time, but you were the only person I thought of . . ."

"No, not at all, what's up?" I countered.

"Well, in my hometown there is this juvenile boys' home that is really in disrepair; I mean, it's a great, important program, the boys are local and can stay near their families. But the building . . . it's a mess and the County wants to tear it down. I don't think they'll replace it with a new facility, either. So, the boys home will get folded into some bigger program somewhere else, I guess," she said, sounding defeated.

"Do you know what's wrong with the building, exactly?" I queried.

"Not really, just that it needs everything! New roof, new flooring, windows, and it doesn't even have air conditioning. Is there a grant for that?"

"Actually, I might have an idea for a way I could help," I said, already scanning my mind for a list of soon-to-open programs my office was monitoring. "Let's set a phone call with them."

It turned out we did find a grant for the boys' home—we succeeded in obtaining $150,000 to rehabilitate the site. Read on to see how we turned Larissa's concerns for the facility—her idea or issue—into a project the GFO could understand.

Once a prospect realizes there is truly grant money available, the tempo of our conversation experiences an uptick. In the early stages, the more people learn about grant funds, the more excited they become. Suddenly, the prospective grant applicant will come upon the notion that maybe their project just won't work, or that maybe it somehow can't fit. The applicant becomes overwhelmed with the options and confused about how to pare them down into a workable set of possible funders to pursue. Questions usually emerge such as these:

"I'm certain that my project is ripe for grant funding. How do I know where to look?"

"Is there a government agency that funds projects like mine?"

"Do charitable foundations care about what I do? Do they offer grants for my work?"

"What are the government agencies with grant money? Is there some sort of special list?"

"My project is a little bit unique. Will anyone be interested in something that isn't mainstream?"

In every case, I do the same as I did with Larissa's concern: We always go back to how we can take a problem, and idea, or a product and turn it into a project (to further our discussion of Step 1 in Chapter 3). Once we know what the project is, we can build it around the grant programs available.

This chapter shows you how to match your idea with the GFO's definition of project. This is a critical step most grant funding books overlook entirely. Once you understand how to interpret the activities that a GFO defines as a project, you'll read grant notices accurately and quickly decide if your idea meets the GFO's definitions and eligibility.

Once you know if you're eligible, you'll be able to efficiently make a decision to go for the grant, or to look for a different opportunity.

TYPES OF WORK YOU CAN FUND WITH GRANTS

GFOs fund nearly any kind of work or project. Just when I make the assumption that "grants just don't fund that sort of thing," I'm proven wrong by some obscure program that does. However, there are certain things that are commonly funded and are easy to find, which is where I'd like to start. GFOs take their own approaches to each category. Some may define the topic very specifically, allowing only a few eligible projects; others will allow a broad definition and be open to many innovative approaches. That is learned through contact with your GFO and from experience. For now, let's get started with the following:

Commonly Funded Project Types:

Business planning
Technical assistance
Research and development
Construction
Workforce development
Working capital
Redevelopment
Professional services
Fees, licensing, and permitting
Equipment
Education and learning
Marketing campaigns

Feasibility studies
Proof of concept
Site expansion
Land acquisition
Community projects
Project management
Cleanup
Grant administration
Curriculum design
Demonstration or pilot-scale
Prevention programs
Developing reference materials

JUMP AHEAD

Move forward to Appendix A: Project Evaluation Tool, after deciding whether your idea fits any of the types of projects you can fund with the grants categories listed here.

WHAT DOES *TECHNICAL ASSISTANCE* MEAN?

I forgot to mention that the list above was written in code. Well, I'm kidding a little, but not entirely. Part of decoding the mystery around grant funding is deciphering the GFO's grant-like terminology. If you don't have a clue how the GFO is using a word, even a common word or phrase like *technical assistance*, you're completely disadvantaged when trying to complete a grant application. Worse yet, not knowing how to define a term the way the GFO uses it could cause your application to be deemed ineligible. That's not the goal; ineligible applications are out of luck until the next grant round. Even if there is a next time, that round could be a year away, or more.

I've created a cheat-sheet in Table 6.1 that compares common grant industry phrases with 'what they really mean'. Here are a few comparisons between the way the grant funding industry uses a word or phrase and what that same word or phrase means to the rest of us. Don't feel bad; back when I was learning the grant industry, I spent a lot of time relearning terms I thought I knew, too!

Please note that the list in Table 6.1 is a short presentation of examples to get you started. You can see there is both overlap and potential for omission and there are many more combinations. Always make the call to your GFO if you are in doubt.

TABLE 6.1 GFO Mystery Words and Phrases

GFO Word/Phrase	Real-World Translation
Technical assistance	Learning equipment, professional services like energy audits, training, developing curriculums/manuals/testing/certification, economic studies
Workforce development	Staffing costs, job training, writing job descriptions, consulting, creating/retaining jobs
Working capital	Operations and maintenance, labor costs, recurring fees to run organizations
Redevelopment	Existing site upgrades, hazardous waste management, strategic planning, greenscapes, urban planning
Grant administration	Management and allocation of grant dollars, contractors, reporting, and compliance

Where did the boys' home fit in this list of topics? Because there were several needs and they overlapped, I sought grants in the project areas of community development, redevelopment, site expansion, construction, cleanup, and equipment. Knowing the real need was to replace old equipment and literally remake the building, I didn't look at grants where construction or equipment weren't some part of the description. Though there were grants out there for improved curriculums and jobs training, things the boys did need, those needs were not immediate enough to merit pursuing until we knew that they could get funding simply to keep the site open.

WHAT'S TRENDING NOW?

Fashions, celebrities, and hairstyles come and go; grants have trends, too. Dollars are tied to programs and missions that matter to those who either make the laws or donate the funds to foundations, so it's natural that available grants reflect a sign of the times. There are those areas that receive what seems like constant funding, such as medical research and youth programs. Yet, there are niches even among these seemingly perpetual topics. For example, the 1980s and 1990s could be characterized as the *DARE era*. It was a period of exceptional spending, donating, and grant making on drug prevention programs for youth. According to the 2013 book, *With Charity for All*, by Ken Stern, DARE received massive amounts of funding, leading to its widespread adoption and the "penetrating of 75 percent of American school districts. At its apex, DARE annually reached thirty-five million children in the United States."[1] The program's success and the estimated $1 billion spent on it led to countless other drug prevention programs and subprograms. Dollars to establish these followed. It's not to say you cannot find funding for a drug-abuse prevention campaign today, but the extreme attention to the topic was at its height during the time period mentioned.

---

1. Ken Stern, *With Charity for All: Why Charities Are Failing and a Better Way to Give* (New York: Doubleday, 2013), 32.

From my perch monitoring the industries of energy, agriculture, and rural development, there were no greater buzzwords in the last decade than *renewable energy* and *energy efficiency*. I've built an entire consulting practice around the acquisition of funding for energy-related projects, be they projects to create energy from a litany of alternative sources or projects to conserve energy when retrofitting existing sites or equipment. The topic is hot and, in many ways, the funders—federal and foundation alike—are driving the green bandwagon.

From my perch in the industries of energy, agriculture, and rural development, there were no greater buzzwords in the last decade than *renewable energy* and *energy efficiency*.

Short List of Hot Topics for GFOs:

- **Health and wellness:** childhood and adult obesity, smoking and alcohol abuse, local foods, food deserts, the connection of farming and consumers, agricultural practices, stress management/effects of stress on quality of life, sleep, and technology overload

- **Energy efficiency:** lighting, vehicles, batteries, corporate energy auditing, heating/cooling, energy use monitoring systems/controls

- **Renewable energy:** bioenergy, wind, solar, hydropower, nuclear, natural gas, biomass

- **Public health:** disease prevention, emerging infectious diseases, emergency management/crisis management technologies, engine emissions reduction

- **Conservation:** water quality, sustainable building, rebuilding species populations, agricultural practices, recycling, landfills, land use, corporate stewardship

- **Local economic development:** rural or urban, including urban redevelopment, affordable housing, cleanup projects, building greenscapes in general, jobs training and job attraction

- **Innovation:** product/technology development of absolutely any concept
- **International development:** including product innova-tions to use in international development, nutrition, waste management, training and education, entrepreneurship, empowerment

Unique Funding Example

In Part One, you read of trade associations offering grants, including the ALA. You might not be surprised to learn that most of the grants given out by the American Lung Association (ALA) each year center around research. But, savvy grant hunters know that sometimes the funding they seek from a GFO is not to be found in the obvious; rather it can be found by knowing the GFO's mission. GFOs take their mission very seriously, and often apply it very broadly. Take this example of funding awarded to the ALA as reported by the April 2012 Environmental News Service:

> In 2011, Congress reauthorized the Diesel Emission Reduction Pro-gram (DERA), and the ALA was a recipient of some of the funds from this program. . . .
>
> In the 2011 DERA grant program, for instance, the American Lung Association of the Upper Midwest was granted $1.3 million to reduce diesel emissions from 331 vehicles using retrofit, repower, and replace-ment strategies.

These dollars went to public and nonprofit private entities, according to EPA's eligibility guidelines for the DERA program. Money was used to replace fleet trucks with CNG-powered (Com-pressed Natural Gas) vehicles, idle-reducing technologies, and other updates that the EPA called "clean diesel." The ALA is not in the fleet truck or idling technology business, but they believed the program advanced their mission of improving air quality to improve health.

For Larissa's project at the juvenile boys' home, we moved from the topic areas identified as possible targets and then began to think about the hot topics agencies wanted to fund within those targets. Because so much of the site was outfitted in old equipment, we settled on energy-efficiency improvement as a hot topic of preference for my searching. It turned out that we did find a grant program through the state that looked like a fit. It worked out and the project was awarded $150,000 for its updates.

Here's a more detailed breakdown of how it worked:

Initial GFO topic areas searched: community development, redevelopment, site expansion, construction, cleanup, and equipment.

GFO topic areas narrowed: construction and equipment.

GFO project area targeted: construction/energy efficiency.

How it met the GFO project definition: The GFO offered grants for communities and businesses to improve energy efficiency by at least 30 percent. Eligible technologies included lighting, heating, cooling, and some others. The site was evaluated by an independent third-party firm that compared the current, outdated equipment with quotes and ratings for new equipment. The analysis demonstrated more than the required minimum of 30 percent energy efficiency increase could be realized with the replacement, making the project eligible to apply.

THE REAL IMPACT: HOW GRANT DOLLARS MEET A NEED

The applicant in the above example needed new everything as the building was very outdated. More importantly, without the new items needed, the community saw the site as a lost cause—they valued the goals and accomplishments of the program, but couldn't afford to keep the building up to codes. By locating funds for the major construction expenses, the home could then seek the required 50 percent match. Some of these matching dollars, that is, dollars not covered by the grant but still required to complete the project, could be in labor and donated services from other organizations in the community. Some of the matching funds had to be in cash. With the addition of the grant, the project's potential for completion was high and that fact enabled the County to approve money to leverage the grant funding awarded. Ultimately, this grant program saved the site from demolition. More importantly, this project allowed a local community program supporting juvenile boys with behavioral problems to continue its work in the local area.

You can accomplish really valuable projects by pursuing a unique spin within a seemingly straightforward grant program.

JUMP AHEAD

If you're ready to look at the major components in a grant application, head to Part Three, where I cover the major application basics.

NON-MONEY REASONS TO ASK FOR MONEY

Harold was the VP of Marketing for a large electrical utility, a role that, oddly enough, also included overseeing renewable energy (RE) development for the organization. I'd known him for several years, but we weren't well acquainted. I did know his utility had an RE deployment goal, and I'd even pitched him some grant funding strategy work, but he never bit on it. I also knew the utility was run by a conservative board of directors that might not like the federal grant funding concept. As they were a financially sound outfit, I also assumed they just didn't need the grant funding. Then, about a year ago, a new guy at the utility called me.

"Harold wants to see you, and he wanted me to tell you that he hasn't been avoiding you for five years, just that he wasn't sure what he was supposed to do with this grant stuff."

"Oh," I said, waiting for the new guy to proceed.

"Yeah, he's got a 'directive' now and told me to get you in the office and under contract right away. How's your schedule next week?"

Intrigued, I took the meeting. Sitting down with Harold and Patrick, his new hire, I settled in.

"Sarah, we've been doing RE projects for a while. I've never taken grant funds for the development we've done," began Harold. "Recently, the board saw a competitor win a grant—it wasn't even that big—maybe a hundred-thousand or so—you did the work, they said. Then they asked why I wasn't working with you and they called me in and reamed me out for thirty minutes about not looking into the opportunity."

Ouch.

"I thought I was doing right by the Board when I avoided 'government handouts,'" Harold continued. "But the Board felt like I wasn't doing right by our customers by not leveraging all opportunities to look for money to lower project costs. Wow, was I shocked!"

I was, too. It turned out that Harold didn't need the money, per se, that is, he didn't need it to make financial projections work or to obtain a line of credit to complete a project. What he needed was to assure the Board that he had turned over every stone to leverage the customer's investment in the utility and, hence, the RE projects they were building. Harold's story is actually rather common in the grant funding marketplace and is easily uncovered when talking about what the organization is really seeking.

SHOULD GRANTS BE USED ONLY WHEN YOU NEED THE MONEY?

The answer to this question is—it depends. I don't think it's always about the money, but I contend that grants should be used responsibly at all times. However, as you will soon learn, one of the many requirements that some agencies impose is financial soundness of the grantee—you can't be broke and win a grant. This is the expectation that the grantee bring matching funds, to cover 80 percent of the project cost, or more. The bottom line is that if you cannot meet the minimum matching requirements, then you may not be a fit for grant funding.

Grant agencies want to see that their money moves initiatives forward. If an applicant's grant proposal demonstrates objectives in line with the GFO's stated goals, regardless of financial need, the GFO may see that project as a benefit. A company that is in such dire straits that without the grant dollars the project will not cash flow is a situation that is often unacceptable to the GFO and as such a grant request won't be funded. Here's an important question: When you apply for a grant, should you do so only because you need money? The answer usually is "maybe." A better version of this question might be, "Is my project able to move forward without the funds and maintain itself when the funds run out?"

The point is, need can be an important reason for funding, and you will learn that some grant organizations require *statements of need* in order to request funding. Further, I've already provided my opinion on using funds responsibly (grants are a privilege, not a right). But, there are other situations where using grants, when still being fiscally responsible, legal, and following the guidelines and advancing the mission of the agency makes sense. Let's look at a few other examples.

> Remember: Grants are a privilege, not a right.

OTHER VALUES OF GRANTS

Here's my short list of other valid and totally acceptable reasons to utilize grant dollars. Using grant dollars should enable you to:

- Leverage funding
- Enhance public relations
- Establish credibility and validity
- Support your causes
- Gain collaborator buy-in
- Demonstrate trustworthiness

To Leverage Funding

Everyone needs leverage—leverage in the case of matching dollars together to make the most of a financing package is a must. This is certainly a good place to consider seeking grant funding. When you have part of the dollars you need to complete the project, particularly some money up front, looking at grants to pay for all or a portion of the balance is worth considering. Not only does the grant agency often award points for sharing with them the total cost, but you can move forward more quickly when you can draw funds from several sources.

The story of Harold's situation at the utility was one of leveraging investment dollars against money coming in from other investments. In his case, they were specifically leveraging member–customer payments and dues, so they took the responsibility of leveraging those dollars very seriously. Sometimes that situation is equally important from a public relations standpoint and to promote goodwill among your peers, board of directors, or other key networks. Take a look at my next point.

To Enhance Public Relations

One way to enhance your image is to use a grant. This is not a marketing strategy. I don't mean to be flippant here, but I do want to share with you that sometimes once you've won a grant, you should certainly take the occasion to publicize the success. You want to be careful how you do it and be conservative in the style of writing you use. (Avoid "Yippee! We've got some of that government money to spend!" I would hope most sensible people wouldn't go that route, though I've seen worse or it wouldn't end up in this book.)

Here is something else I'll point out while we are on the topic of PR: Never take PR for granted when you are seeking grants. Public perception gets pretty critical when you are using money that is shared by your peers. More than a few of my highest-quality entrepreneur-developed potential projects, which could have made a very positive public impact, were sunk in the court of public opinion. Picture yourself as the developer in this scenario:

Envision a historic urban neighborhood in a midsized Midwestern city where large homes nestle along windy driveways that meander back into wooded lots of an acre or more. It's prime near-downtown real estate. Now picture a spring evening and a community gathering. There are cheerleaders from a couple of local public high schools and local leaders from the city and county councils. Neighbors are

> Never take PR for granted when you are looking for grants.

interested in the general goings-on and are peering at the activity as they walk their dogs.

Now, some polished-looking new folks arrive with an additive technology that will (they say) improve the local environment and the local water quality by reducing the wastewater discharged into the aging downtown infrastructure. All they need is the board of zoning to approve the new installation of this special feature at the plant. The plant has been there a while; it's basically located in the heart of the residential area and the community grew up around it.

On closer inspection, you see the cheerleaders aren't holding pompoms—they're holding placards with nasty phrases urging the project developers to get out. The neighbors aren't just gathering for coffee and dog walking, either. On second glance they appear agitated, and many of them are passing out picket signs. The signs don't make sense, though. They say things like:

"No more smell here!"

"Take your waste out of our water!"

"Don't poison our children with your junk!"

But, that's all misinformation! The project will actually reduce odor, cut down on bacteria, and use only a tiny portion of public funding to make a world of difference in an aging system that could go bust any day! The developers have the testing to prove it!

By the evening's end, the zoning board has been swayed, and the people have spoken. No approval stamp for this entrepreneur. The year-and-a-half and the six figures they've spent in legal and permitting fees is not going to matter here. It's on to a new town or back to the drawing board. Any grants they applied for will be forfeited.

To Establish Credibility and Viability

For those of you developing new products or any technologies, being validated is paramount and stands right up there with cash in terms of true value. There are a number of grants, including those through the Small Business Innovation and Research (SBIR) program (www.sbir.gov) exclusively offered to small businesses to move from concept to commercialization. For instance, Sokikom, an educational web-based game program and former SBIR program awardee, was able to raise over $1 million from private investors after going through SBIR-funded early stage research. For more grant programs and project examples awarded through SBIR and its counterpart, STTR, see the www.sbir.gov website.[2]

Many developers find themselves in the disheartening gap between having the funds to conduct pre-commercial work and having the validity in their concept to seek investors. So, SBIR, STTR, and other small business research grants can enable this process. There are grants that can enable this process and will help entrepreneurs pair their hard work and innovation with the next step to a real business model.

To Support Your Causes

Do you give money to nonprofits? What causes do you believe in? If you had time, dollars, and staffing to move the missions of your favorite causes forward, would you do that?

Entrepreneurs tend to be strong advocates and love giving back. Using grant funds is one avenue. Besides applying for grants to your own foundation or to set up an organization, consider taking the grant money of the organizations you support. Does that sound backwards? It's not. If you have the capacity to help them implement their missions with projects you want to do, then apply for grant dollars from the groups where you give. Those grants exist to help the organization further its objectives, so don't be shy about finding

---

2. Edward Metz, "IES/ED SBIR Awardee Receives Investment Funding to Launch," SBIR/STTR, http://sbir.gov/news/iesed-sbir-awardee-receives-investment-funding-launch (May 5, 2013).

a project that makes sense and requesting the funds to imple-ment it. In effect, use their money so you can spread their word. Here is one thing to be aware of—be certain you agree with that mission! Remember, any time you accept the dollars from any agency, you are literally endorsing that agency's position.

> Remember, any time you accept the dollars from any agency, you are literally endorsing that agency's position.

To Gain Collaborator Buy-In

Sometimes a project you wish to build needs a group of stakeholders to agree before it gets up and running. Consider the case of an East Coast university I worked with in recent years. The Office of the President created a "sustainability goal"—whatever that meant was anyone's guess. The program didn't have many parameters and department heads were generally confused about it. Taking the initiative, however, the operations department decided to advance the notion by installing biomass-powered boilers to heat and cool campus buildings. The entrepreneur who designed the bioenergy system and who had already spent several months collaborating with the university's operational managers contacted me. They loved the idea. My client was proactive in many ways. For example, he'd also worked with local economic development groups to source the biomass (in this case, wood waste from the surrounding forestry industry) needed for the boilers to make renewable power. This "feedstock" was now a value-added item rather than a waste with an added cost to be landfilled.

So, when he and the operations team approached the president's office they were shocked to hit a brick wall. The president said no, saying he liked the idea but, being located in a city known for "community action," as he called it, he was quite worried that the public wouldn't like the project. The president cited horror stories of activist groups claiming "deforestation" due to energy projects and didn't want any part of that fanfare. Besides, the president said, their city was finding it notoriously difficult to obtain permitting for new projects, especially those near historic areas, such as the landmark-heavy downtown district the university occupied. Finally, there was the multimillion-dollar cost that the president said he just wasn't willing to push through the channels.

Stalled, but determined to implement his technology, the entrepreneur-developer found his way to my office. We discussed his concerns, realizing it ultimately boiled down to a lack of collaborator and stakeholder buy-in, driven partially by money and partially by a lack of knowledge. We decided that he needed to show the president that others in the community bought into the project. Fortunately, I had worked in the state before and knew that they had a fund of money specifically set aside to help advance economic development in certain economically challenged areas of the state. Now, the city was not on the map of approved regions, but I was looking farther down the line for funding since the grant program also targeted agricultural products. When we reviewed where he was sourcing his woody "feedstock" for the new boilers, it turned out those areas qualified.

We contacted a few state agencies and found they had a competitive grant fund for agribusiness projects. At first glance, boilers on an urban college campus don't seem like an agribusiness project, but by applying for the funding based on the *source* of the project's inputs, that is, the woody biomass, we fit. Quickly bringing in the operations team from the university, they agreed to ask the president to sit down with the state agency and talk about possibly applying for the funds. The available dollars were fairly significant in that up to a couple of million was allocated over several years. We knew that would get the president's attention and he agreed. We also brought the state's permitting agency to the table. Once the discussion was over, the project had a go-ahead from the president, a new lease on life, and a solid opportunity for several millions in grant dollars.

To Demonstrate Trustworthiness

Admittedly, this particular category is a little tarnished by fairly recent developments in the federal funding area—including the many failed projects that have received national press attention. However, if done correctly, there is still a great deal of truth behind this reason for seeking grants. I think this is especially true in the case of nongovernment-funded sources.

Take the example of funding offered by trade groups. If your trade organization backs a new technology and provides funding to that entity to complete research or deployment, does that give you a measure of trust in the product of the system your membership group supported? Yes, cynics will wonder who had their palms greased, and I understand that jaded sort of thinking in business, but go ahead, really consider it. Does knowing someone on the board of directors who reviewed the material personally and worked collaboratively with other peers of yours to approve funding make the funded project a little more honest or legitimate to you? Depending on the organization, it might. I work with several trade organizations that offer grants to members and nonmembers aiming to further the association's mission. Take a look at your technology, your product, your service or system. If you haven't already, at least research what trade groups are out there representing people—including your competitors. Do they have money to invest?

Pairing with a respected association is absolutely in the win column for an entrepreneur seeking to be seen as trustworthy in the marketplace.

PERSPECTIVES ON PROSPERITY

> When I chased after money, I never had enough. When I got my life on purpose and focused on giving of myself and everything that arrived into my life, then I was prosperous.
>
> —*Dr. Wayne Dyer*

The best systems and approaches are those designed organically. These are processes that appear out of the creativity born of necessity and are honed over time until they work seamlessly in nearly every circumstance.

This quote from Wayne Dyer illustrates that when you move an important project forward, you accomplish much more than financial gain. I encourage you to seek unique funding sources for unique projects. Grant funding may be that source, but it's not just about the money, as you've read in this chapter. Grant funding can be used by entrepreneurs and business—not simply for research and development. Hot areas for grant funding include:

- Energy
- Sustainability
- Food safety
- General health and wellness
- Innovation in nearly any segment
- International development, particularly in agriculture and health care

Yet, besides funding important projects, grant dollars can serve a larger purpose for both the recipient and the GFO looking to award funds. Grant money moves missions forward and helps accomplish big objectives. It can also establish credibility for the recipient and help build a positive public image for an important project.

Securing money from any source is essential when you've got to have it. However, focusing too much on what you want and how much money you need is no way to win grant awards. Highlight the multiple features and benefits to others in your applications. When you share with the GFO how many people gain from your work, you are exponentially more likely to be funded. When you get funded, the good works you can do and the missions you can endeavor to promote are limitless.

CHAPTER SEVEN

The High Stakes of Winning or Losing Grants

You've just figured out that you've got a lot riding on this decision to apply for grants. Thinking through this is part of the process.

Joe was a great business developer. He possessed all the qualities that true believers need to make something happen. He was passionate about his project's intent and value, organized in the way he described and presented the benefits of his project and best of all, he really got it when we worked through the requirements to prepare for a grant. He had become my model client and my staff loved working with him. One day he called, fretting. Being just days ahead of the deadline, this sort of anxiety is normal. Like most big projects, there is invariably a glitch that causes everyone to lose hair and sleep. While I didn't enjoy the deadline-crunch problems that came up, I was used to them. I have to be since applicants aren't.

But, Joe wasn't worried about the grant preparation process.

"Sarah, how is winning this grant going to affect my marriage? I think it could be in real trouble here, or at least I'm looking at weeks on the sofa!"

"Huh? Pardon me?" was all I could muster at first. His marriage? This one proved I hadn't seen it all.

"My wife and I have been debating about federal spending and the so-called fiscal cliff and all that 'stimulus money' that's been awarded. She told me that she is seriously against using government money for, well, anything, I think. She thinks its nuts to give entrepreneurs money for improvement projects. She just watched some piece about a failed project that was awarded an enormous loan guarantee."

"Joe, you've surely told her that you're applying for a federal grant, right?" I asked, concerned that I knew his answer.

"Heck, no! I mean, I planned to eventually, but I just didn't realize that she was so political about this. What should we do?" The frantic tone of Joe's voice rose to a crescendo.

We?

Joe's story is not a unique example for me. Believe it or not, I've "counseled" more than a few couples through differing points of view about accepting grant dollars in their businesses. It's a fair fight—as you know, I'm not writing this book to convince you that foundations, corporations, or governments should or should not offer grant money. You're welcome to debate that around your own dinner table. But, I will ask you: Do you want a grant? If you do, be ready for these kinds of conversations because they will emerge in the strangest of places. I've created this chapter just so that you have a little preparation for the question: "Just because I can, does it mean I should?"

I cannot answer that for you, nor could I for Joe. What I can say is that you've got to be aware of some of the ramifications that exist if you apply for a grant and win it. I've had this conversation around fancy boardroom tables in 38th-floor corporate offices; I've discussed the issue over the bed of a pickup truck. I've even penciled out the pros and cons of accepting grant funding on a bar napkin in a questionably safe tavern. No applicant of any size or sophistication is immune to this issue. Before you have to sleep on the couch or handle damage control in the marketplace, ask Joe's question: How does wining a grant affect your relationships?

The third step in the prosperity process is Ponder, as seen in Figure 7.1. Ponder is the guidepost for this chapter. We're just about three-quarters of the way through learning enough about grants to make a solid "are-we-in-or-out" decision. In the next chapter, we begin to move into application preparation tips; I know you are itching to get started. But, spend the time on Step 3; you may regret it if you don't.

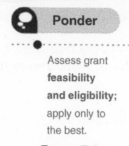

FIGURE 7.1

Ponder

Source: Created by Brandrenew.

Deborah S. Koch, author of *How to Say It: Grantwriting, Write Proposals that Grant Makers Want to Fund*,[1] offers the following advice in her 2009 book: "In grant seeking, words can go where you can't—a government program officer's desk, a foundation boardroom, a corporation's headquarters—so you want to use them as the strategic, powerful tools that they are." I agree and this chapter is all about formulating that strategy for a successful proposal.

As I've been writing this book like a one-on-one conversation, think of this chapter as our full-day strategy session with your team. If you are not certain who the team members are at this point, jump ahead to Chapter 8 for an overview of team member selection and the role of a project manager specific to grant assembly. Carefully evaluate the topics presented ahead and you'll be ready to handle just about any situation of concern relative to your acceptance of grant funding.

JUMP AHEAD

For more information on creating a project team, jump ahead to Chapter 8, where I provide an overview of team member selection and the role of a project manager specific to grant assembly.

---

1. Deborah S. Koch, *How to Say It: Grantwriting*, 1st ed. (New York, Prentice Hall Press, 2009).

STRATEGIC CONSIDERATIONS BEFORE APPLYING

Here are the seven broadly defined strategic considerations I encourage all grant applicants to work through before applying for funding:

1. Alignment of mission and vision
2. Financial considerations
3. Public relations/marketplace impact
4. Privacy and intellectual capital exposure
5. Personal and social ramifications
6. Added costs
7. Timing

Alignment of Mission and Vision

Endorsement, promotion, alignment—these are all words that you embody when you, in effect, partner with the GFO by accepting its funds.

You know whenever you've woken up with a crick in your neck that it's a bad feeling to be out of alignment. That's what it might feel like down the road if your goals and views don't mesh with the GFO. Resolving this issue is my first priority for applicants. When you consider a GFO for funding, understand what that organization stands for in the world. Do you know how it was founded and on what principles? Do you know its political leanings and are those similar enough to yours that you can honestly say you'll endorse this program publically with your participation? Even though it's your project, it's the GFO's money and the organization sees you as advancing its mission in the world or it would not have made the award. Are you supportive or squeamish?

Take the occasion to know the company you keep. I doubt you'll have the opportunity to meet the political appointee who sits at the head of a government agency—but you might. How would you feel if he or she gave a stump speech at your place of business? Politics can quickly change at the federal level, but might do so more slowly in corporate and foundation programs. In this world, pay special attention to other awardees. Would you want to network with these people at a conference?

Consider the issue Jenn ran into when she applied for a grant without looking at the agency's annual giving report.

"I nearly freaked out reading the morning paper today," Jenn exclaimed when I ran into her at a meeting. "That foundation grant that I applied for, you know, the one with the $150,000 to start a youth program for my boss's foundation?" I nodded, and she went on: "Well, apparently that group donates a couple million bucks a year to the most liberal anti–fossil fuel lobby on the continent! I just read that they're part of a group behind a series of new anti-drilling commercials. What am I going to do?"

Here's the background on the problem: Jenn's boss was a prominent shareholder in cooperative operating oil and gas distribution. He was wealthy and was planning to run for office in a few years. He had just hired her away from the mayor's office to help him build his philanthropic interests, which would include some grant-writing work.

"It's okay," I began, sitting down with Jenn on a bench. "Contact the agency and simply withdraw your application. I'd go a step further and ask them if you can pick up the materials you sent or if they'd return them to you COD."

"Should I tell my boss I applied for a very *wrong* grant?"

I wasn't touching that one.

Eventually, Jenn's boss hired my firm not only to research funding opportunities, but also to vet potential GFO fits for conflicts with his goals and core values. Jenn worked with me to write the grants after that, but we were certainly careful in our selection of where to apply!

Financial Considerations

Not being a financial, tax, or legal expert, I'm going to keep this section brief but with an important message: Find out your legal, tax, and financial implications if you receive a grant award. Grants are

Once you sign the grant agreement, you are to adhere to a legally binding contract—you'll want the best advice you can obtain to review that agreement with you.

potentially considered taxable income. You should seek to understand that possibility with your advisors. Once you sign the grant agreement, you are to adhere to a legally binding contract—you'll want the best advice you can obtain to review that agreement with you. Financially, receiving a grant may be a positive on the balance sheet, but examine its potential effect on your ability to qualify for other financing. Talk about these possibilities early in the process.

Public Relations/Marketplace Impact

Some people believe all press is good press. This is the notion that as long as somebody is talking about them, they're doing something right. If you're in that camp, this section may not matter to you. However, if you're more concerned with your position in the marketplace, read on.

Many applicants ask me if they have to publically disclose their acceptance of a grant award. Check with the aforementioned advisers, first, to see if you have any conflicts of interest if you don't. Beyond that, it depends on the grant program. I work with a number of federal programs that require portions of your application to be public during review. Most of these cases involve large commercial building projects and the environmental and zoning reviews that accompany them. In these instances, applicants may have to put a notice in the paper—more than once—and even have physical copies of application components on display at a local public place such as a library or town hall. Be aware this will stall the grant review/acceptance process 30 to 60 days while these are left for the public's comment. Not all situations are as invasive as this example, but that doesn't mean your award will be private. The GFO is likely required to make some kind of public notice listing its grant awardees. In that case, while you may not have to disclose anything separately, your name may still be in the paper or at least on the GFO's website. No, it's not going to be as obvious as Publishers Clearinghouse arriving at your door with a huge check, Ed McMahon's replacement, 50 balloons, and a camera crew. But there might be some kind of fanfare involved.

> It's not going to be as obvious as Publishers Clearinghouse arriving at your door with a huge check, but there might be some kind of fanfare involved.

Find out what the GFO has in mind.

JUMP AHEAD

Jump ahead to Chapter 11, where I discuss possible publicity that the GFO may require or encourage once you've won an award.

Privacy and Intellectual Capital Exposure

Researchers often apply for grants to fund time and materials to prove concepts. However, at what cost? What do you give away when you accept a grant? Do you give away your intellectual capital? Are your business or process secrets automatically published on some website, free to download by everyone? What is exposed? These questions all go back to the grant agreement. Ask the GFO about any concerns you have on trademark, intellectual capital, and ownership of your project up front. There may be negotiating room here, even with federal programs, so ask for what you need.

Once you find out what you give up and what you don't, then weigh the risk. Some entrepreneurs don't want any information about their project in the public domain. In this case, grants are likely a poor choice for their financing needs. Alternatively, small businesses needing to prove concept to move from demonstration to commercialization may be looking at a project that happens because of the funding or an idea that dies without it. It's all in your perspective and it is a very individual decision.

Personal and Social Ramifications

I have received calls from unfunded applicants demanding to know why my office didn't do as good a job on their application as we did for their neighbor's application the year before. I don't like the way a conversation like this begins. Rolling with it, I remind these applicants that we didn't guarantee funding since we don't evaluate the grants once submitted. Now, I realize that is not what they called to hear, but, I've had these talks enough times to know what is going on. In industries where everybody knows each other and the grant program is around year after year, word of "who's gotten what and how much" gets around. Nobody likes to feel like they've somehow been slighted, even though everyone's situation is different. I've also been asked why I didn't select an applicant for funding. Again, I try to explain that I don't get the option to do so; however, sometimes, disappointed people just need someone to blame.

Even if your neighbor was never denied for the same grant that you've received, be prepared for a few hints of jealousy if you win an award. If you've ever lost a lot of weight or "had some work done" you probably noticed a few of your friends treated you differently. Winning grants can be like that! Your professional peers (and your neighbors, too) may grumble about the supposed preferential treatment you received. Politics have an interesting way of coming up at this point, too, so watch out for that whammy rearing its ugly head at the neighborhood barbeque. If the agency's position aligns with their own, I find most applicants don't mind dealing with some basic pettiness on other people's part because they stand behind their decision to apply. However, if you are a public figure or are in the middle of some kind of personal or professional trial, it might not be the right time to attract more attention by winning a grant award.

Added Costs

If you hire a grant consultant there is an added cost. I wrote this book for those of you who want to consider working on grants independently, so those expenses may be limited. However, there are other expenses in making a grant application. The most significant cost could be in the pre-work you are required to include in the application—some of it may be perfectly necessary for the project to pencil out and as such isn't really an added cost of grant seeking. For instance, financial plans, business, plans, pro formas, site surveys, and tax returns are normal costs of doing business. However, the grant agency may require other aspects that you weren't necessarily planning for in your budget. Now you have to decide if this added cost is worth the money. When clients ask me what I think, I encourage them to look at it two ways. First, decide if the added work—be it a formal feasibility study or perhaps a market survey conducted by an independent firm—is worth anything to you in any other capacity. If you could use that material to help yourself be a better entrepreneur or as documentation for other funding sources, it might be worth the cost. Second, you need to look at how often you'll use these added requirements. Are you planning to apply for additional grants where these kinds of things are a necessity?

Added costs from grants also come in the form of compliance. One of the biggest areas for compliance is labor law. Your contractors and their vendors may be subject to certain wage minimums or additional safety compliance. These additional costs are sure to be passed on to you, making the quotes you receive for work higher than if the vendor wasn't required to comply with a grant request. Does the added cost still make sense or would it be cheaper to go without the grant?

JUMP AHEAD

Jump ahead to Chapter 9 for the list of major application components, including potential supporting documentation and addendums you may need to acquire in advance of grant application.

Compliance and reporting are also required post-award. Sometimes reporting is minimal and in other cases it can be quite laborious. Here are some questions I pose to applicants:

- Do you have time to handle the reporting requirements?
- If not, what is the cost of a project manager or grant administrator?
- Does this expense make receiving a grant less appealing?

Timing

Application decisions often hinge on the issue of award and payment timing. I concur that the question of when you'll receive the funding is essential to know. There are a couple of frustrations in this section, though, so beware. First, notice of your award or denial status can be a long or a short wait time. I've worked with programs that provided a yes answer in less than a week while others have taken 18 months or more. There is certainly no standard award wait time; it's program specific. How does that wait affect your project's progress?

Second, while the agency will often list an anticipated award date in the NOFA, they won't always stick with it. That's very irksome, I know, but it happens fairly often. In the programs I work with regularly, I can usually tell an applicant how likely it is that the GFO will stick with the publicized schedule. Yet, I can still be wrong. We're not in charge of the timing and that is a fact.

The final issue to cover is about timing deals with disbursement of funding. You must know whether the grant works as a reimbursement or if any of the funding is paid up front upon award. Also, how are those dollars paid to you and in how many installments over how many months or years? The agency should be willing to go over these details; I would ask.

JUMP AHEAD

Jump Ahead to Chapter 11 for a discussion of how and when you may be paid following grant award. This chapter also includes common reporting requirements and templates for documenting your post-award procedures.

WHEN TO PARTNER ON AN APPLICATION

Knowing you are entrepreneurs, I realize many readers won't have the desire to partner on anything when it involves sharing money! I get that and I'm not suggesting that grant funding requires partnerships to acquire. It does not. However, let's say your project type appears to be eligible for a grant, but the GFO tends to award only nonprofits or communities for the work you seek to do. Sharing the grant award with an eligible applicant is a possibility. Or, what if you just cannot complete the project alone under the potential grant terms and really need a hand? I've developed a list outlining scenarios where partnerships might offer a solution that will take you from turning away an opportunity to winning it.

Possible Partnership Situations:
- Where partnering enables applicant eligibility
- If more than one participant is required by the GFO
- If you need more matching dollars than you can obtain alone
- If the partnership strengthens your application in any way
- If it improves your application's score
- When you improve or enable access to equipment, staff, sites, or services you otherwise could not afford for the grant work

If you do partner, all the pieces we discussed in the strategic considerations should be worked through together before application. This is especially important if the organization is structured differently from yours, such as pairing an academic institution with a small business. This partnership arrangement is not uncommon, but challenges emerge because of the speed at which the different entities can react.

Finally, be certain to consider which partner is handling

Consider carefully the percentage of award each applicant receives and put this in the grant application and agreement. If you are not the sole applicant, be clear about how much money goes to each participant.

> Universities take as much as 85 percent of the funding from faculty members applying.

the cash. If you're handling the money, does that entail contractors for the work or can the GFO handle that? Also, consider carefully the percentage of award each applicant receives and put this in the grant application and agreement. If you are not the sole applicant, be clear about how much money goes to each participant.

Partnerships between academia and private sector look great to GFOs, but universities take as much as 85 percent of the funding from faculty members applying. For that reason, your academic partner may want a higher share than you expected since she knows the actual amount of money she has to spend is deeply discounted. How does that sit with you?

Please, have these conversations now, not after grant award!

DO SPECIAL CERTIFICATIONS MATTER?

You will find preferential treatment or even eligibility based on some kind of "special status." This category, which includes preferential status for race, gender, nationality, income level, and even project type, is very broad. The federal government offers certain applicants unique eligibility, additional points on the application, or added priority in some of their programs, but not all. For example, I've done federal grant applications where young or beginning farmers received more points, giving them a score advantage. Some GFOs provide priority funding to applicants in pre-identified cities and counties with low-income levels by national standards. Eligibility could be determined by the place of performance for your project. For example, USDA's business programs grants require the project site be located in a rural area. Paraphrasing the regulation, it specifies that projects be located only in a community of 50,000 or less and not adjacent to a larger community that doesn't meet the definition. The agency even has a website where the exact address can be entered to confirm acceptance. Literally, the possibilities for special designations or personal or professional status are endless. Once you navigate the grant scene for a while, you'll see some of these continue to emerge. Grant hunting around a specific status is also a good idea and may yield results. You may also find websites and trade groups geared toward aiding defined groups of applicants with grant funding.

I am often asked if I recommend becoming certified in a certain program, such as the Women's Business Enterprise (WBE) program. I do recommend such certifications, but not necessarily for grant hunting. My company holds WBE status at the national level and in my home state of Indiana. I am also a Certified Woman-Owned Small Business (WOSB). I want to point out that these kinds of certifications are rarely required for grant funding; rather they are more likely to be used with government or corporate contracting for professional services and products that the business offers. To learn more about certifications, visit the following websites:

- Women's Business Enterprise: http://www.wbenc.org/
- Government Contract Services: http://www.simplegsa.com/ contact-us/?_vsrefdom=gaw&gclid=CP32jo3BpbcCFf E7MgodPV8AyA

PERSPECTIVES ON PROSPERITY

Thinking of your new venture critically yet creatively will allow you to uncover the fresh grass of prosperity and potential under the blanket of snow.

——*Sarah Beth Aubrey*, The Profitable Hobby Farm: How to Build a Sustainable Local Foods Business

This quote comes from my second book, *The Profitable Hobby Farm*, published in 2010 by a Wiley imprint, Howell Book House. In this quote, I was speaking directly to entrepreneurs urging them to seek balance in the passion and excitement that they bring to each new venture. I was encouraging strategic thinking then as I do now.

So, to recap the key concepts in this chapter, here again are my top seven strategic considerations for grant funding:

1. Alignment of mission and vision
2. Financial considerations

3. Public relations/marketplace impact
4. Privacy and intellectual capital exposure
5. Personal and social ramifications
6. Added costs
7. Timing

Each of these can have a high cost—especially if overlooked or done incorrectly. The strategic implications that accompany acceptance of a grant are yet another reason why grants are never free.

CHAPTER EIGHT

Creating a Project Team

> Pulling together a unified grant from a team of individuals can be like pulling teeth. There must be a way to make it easier.

"Sarah, believe me, I'm as absolutely furious about this as you are," began my colleague, a mature professional named Bill whom I respected. "Honestly, I'm really torn up about it, especially since it was the first project we've endeavored to work on together," he added.

Said project was an RFP response that would have become a mutual client, had there not been the screw-up we were discussing.

"How did it happen, Bill? He missed the deadline?" I queried, still incredulous that an established firm like Bill's would make such a pedestrian mistake.

"Yes, apparently Johnny laid the submission packet on Tonya's desk on Friday afternoon before he left. He intended that she FedEx it, but he didn't realize she was out that day," he admitted, a bit sheepishly.

"Who cares whether she was out, Bill; it was Johnny's responsibility to this team to get the grant submitted. To hand it off to someone else he didn't even communicate with . . . " I paused. I was unnerved to be pushing Bill so hard. He was a mentor, and I was younger, less experienced, and had a staff of two-and-a-half to his 40-some. But, this was amateurish. I continued: "And, sending on a Friday when the deadline is Monday—having it sit somewhere over the weekend? Bill, that wasn't a responsible idea, anyway."

"Yeah, I know, we put a reprimand in his file, but, what can I say at this point? The opportunity is lost."

THE PROJECT TEAM

This story illustrates the importance of project team selection. The role each person plays impacts the success of the overall quality. Yes, it can affect your chances to win the grant. In a business of deadlines, particularly nonnegotiable ones, missing one is *never* an option. That being the case, the person responsible for submission of the grant had better be the most responsible person you know. What happened at Bill's company? In my view, he put the wrong person in charge of essential work. That individual didn't own his role all the way through. Here was a young project team member who assumed sending a package was the job of a secretary, not the job of a budding junior executive like himself. I'd met plenty of "Johnnys" before. His view: Friday afternoon was time to head out for the weekend, not worry over the mail when his important role was done. So, what part of the role should Bill or I have owned? Did we screw this up as much as Johnny the Flippant? I think we did. If Johnny had better understood that he carried the ball for the project, and that if he dropped it, all work was for naught, maybe he would have cared to have more follow-through. That's Bill's job, I suppose. Maybe I should have offered to handle the submission, or at least called to make certain it had been done correctly. *That* was my job. Everybody screwed up this opportunity—and, as Bill said, it was lost.

Knowing how to assemble a grant application team takes finesse. This portion of grant funding is both strategic planning and application preparation. It includes assigning roles, timeliness, duties, and amassing the required materials. Project teams could make assessments about the eligibility and feasibility of the grant application, review the work, make judgments as to what is important to include, and determine the ramifications on the organization. The combination of strategy and tactics is why I include this topic here. This chapter and Chapter 9 together are the bridge between the thinking and the doing.

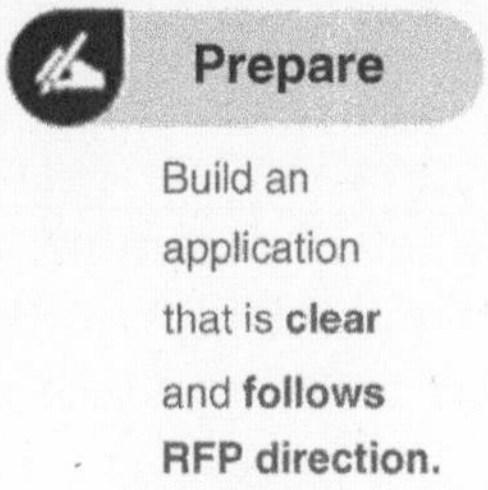

 Prepare

Build an
application
that is **clear**
and **follows**
RFP direction.

FIGURE 8.1

Prepare

Source: Created by Brandrenew.

In this and a few of the following chapters, we will work through Step 4 of the Prosperity Process: Prepare. See Figure 8.1.

You may find it interesting that I consider the actual grant application preparation as the next-to-last step in winning a grant. Having gone through two-thirds of my book, you

> I firmly believe most grant funding opportunities are best passed by.

now see why. I firmly believe most grant funding opportunities are best passed by, so I've spent a great deal of this book talking about how to select your best shot.

Once you've come to that decision, it's time to build a power-house application. You will see a number of roles in the following chapter material. There is no reason to assign a different person to each role—certainly you don't need a 20-person team even for the largest of applications. However, all the roles need to be filled. Knowing in advance the importance of each function keeps applicants on target and reduces the possibility that something will be overlooked.

JUMP AHEAD

Go to Chapter 9 to learn about what's included in a grant application. Chapter 10 covers unique ways to improve your application's success.

IMPORTANCE OF A SOLID TEAM

The GFOs receipt of your complete grant application is a base minimum, assuming you select a team member with more concern for the project than Johnny the Flippant. But, deadline duds aren't the only way your project team members can make or break your grant funding request.

Project team members are your partners. They may be partners only while you prepare the application or they may be co-applicants with you who will be sharing in the grant award. Regardless of the duration, choose these individuals carefully. It is for that reason that I feel that the selection of partnerships is strategic. You must determine what each partner brings to the table. Is it money you need and they bring matching funds? Is it a different tax status you need and they are organized as a not-for-profit when you are a for-profit entity? Do they bring expertise, or more people to conduct the work or trials, or does your potential partner have a greater measure of pull with the GFO than you? All of these reasons may be valid. Knowing what they bring is important, but it still can't exclusively make the decision. Think even broader: What is your partner's role in the marketplace? Do you share the same values and missions? If you don't, preparing the application and coming to agreement on how things are said may be impossible. Or, if you win the grant, allocating the funds could prove a challenge if you believe in one set of ideals and your partner another. Politics do matter, and if potential partners are polar opposites, you could have a mess. I also encourage my applicants to consider project team members for inclusion based upon their workloads and the pace at which they complete tasks. No matter who is on the team, you'll have to accept certain caveats when you partner with an organization that operates at a different speed than you do. Are they known for being expedient or for missing deadlines? Is the potential partner's organization stable or constantly rotating employees? Are their team members or partners willing to negotiate and compromise, or are they known for being difficult? Finally, if you do add contractors to the project, vet them in advance, even if the timeline is tight. Along those lines, I'll share an unpleasant story.

I was working with a client to review a grant application within 30 days following GFO's suggestions to improve it. The GFO liked the project and gave us the time to meet additional criteria they believed would make it stronger when presented to the full technical committee. One suggestion had been to add a different third-party reviewer. In this case, the agency felt the PE (professional engineer) we had used for the technical review was too close to the project, and they asked for an additional party to sign off on the project. My client had recently attended an industry tradeshow and returned with the contact number for a PE in Kentucky. I didn't know him, but we ended up contracting with him since the notice was tight. Immediately things were disastrous. He blew through deadlines, never responded to e-mails without constant hounding, and missed scheduled conference calls. We waited, and waited, and waited for his first draft. Several days in a row he would e-mail to indicate it would just be a few more days. Then, he stopped e-mailing. Then, he stopped taking calls. Two days before the deadline, I called the GFO, head hanging, trying to figure out a way to beg them to let us extend at this short notice. I received a stroke of amazing luck: My agency contact actually knew of the wayward PE. He'd heard of him because another applicant had experienced the same trouble we had. The contact informed us that said contractor had even lost his license. Thankfully, he offered us another 30 days. I won't count on that happening twice in my career, but I was grateful for it that day.

JUMP AHEAD

To learn about what is required in grant reporting, see Chapter 11.

SELECTING A PROJECT MANAGER

The most important role in a successful grant application is the project manager.

A gathering of dynamic and brilliant individuals does not make a team. Great people coming together can still be a disjointed mess without good organization. Along with their expertise, team members

The most important role in a successful grant application is the project manager.

bring their baggage—their agenda, timeline, and schedules, the pulls from other priorities, and their unique work style—to a project that's probably already on too-tight a deadline. Besides that, your objective as a team is to take the possible varied combinations of technical data, quotes, vendor bios, curriculums, financials, budgets, timelines, surveys, and reports and create a convincing narrative package that meets the guidelines, works out in a realistic budget, satisfies a review from each player who brought a piece to the project, and gets submitted on time. It's a lot to ask.

Your team needs a lead person—a quarterback, you could say. The project manager may serve several roles. I certainly covered multiple roles at once when I was newer in business and had more time and less accessible expertise to hire. I still write and review grants today, but I always have at least one other person who does the "manufacturing."

Here are some possible roles a good grant project manager should fill:

- Undisputed Leader—where the buck stops
- Writer—or good enough writer/editor to review the grant writer's work
- Researcher
- Fact checker
- Authority on grant eligibility and feasibility
- Grant submitter
- GFO contact
- Responsible for acquiring/vetting documentation
- Able to source additional expertise or contractors, if needed
- Critical reviewer, able to identify problems to fix and positives to play up

- Content merger—ability to formulate everyone's expertise into one document with a consistent style
- Meeting coordinator
- Timeline enforcer
- Assigner of roles within the team
- Responsible party/project owner

The most important function of the project manager is to care about the success of the grant application and make sure that what needs to happen does happen, without question. Missing deadlines is *not* an option.

I once flew to Washington, D.C. the day an application was due because FedEx kept missing the GFO's building location. On a massive federal agency building spanning about three city blocks, the driver could not seem to find the correct door to make delivery even though we had tripled-checked the address. We had even sent the package overnight, three days in advance (which is plenty tight, in my view), paid the high price, and they still were not going to make delivery on time. At 11:00 A.M. on the due date, we were told the next attempt wouldn't be until 3:30 P.M. They suggested we hire a courier to intercede, but the package was en-route with a driver and he wouldn't return to a pickup location until 2:30 P.M. I wasn't having this problem on my head. My staff and I ran off new copies, bought me a plane ticket, and I hand-delivered it by 3:30 P.M. with one hour to spare. That grant was for big money—my client didn't mind the additional expense when their award letter arrived.

SHOULD I HIRE A GRANT WRITER?

This is an extremely important question for most applicants. As the audience for this book is entrepreneurs, I'll answer the question differently for you than for other groups with whom I dialog. If you are extremely busy, overcommitted, not knowledgeable about the grant funding world, have trouble staying on deadline, are managing multiple projects that require travel or your attention for long periods of time, or simply want the grant but don't want to complete all the work, then I think you should. The question, then, is what kind of grant professional do you need? The following provides a few options.

I believe there are two types of grant professionals available to contract: grant preparers and grant consultants. Both have a fit, and you may at one time use a grant preparer and at another seek a consultant. Here's my breakdown of the roles each can play.

Grant-Preparer Roles:
- Writer
- Materials preparer
- Researcher
- Reviewer/editor
- Possible submitter
- Agency contact
- Reporting or administration after award
- Less likely to advise
- Typically complies with direction set by applicant

Note that this professional is usually obtained at a lower hourly wage than a consultant and possibly without a retainer. Experience is still essential; this role does not necessarily imply a junior- or administrative-level individual. However, keep in mind that this professional probably won't advise on strategic direction. If you need that aspect, you need a grant consultant.

Grant Consultant Roles:
- Offers services to cover everything grant preparer does
- Full project manager (see project manager roles)
- Strategic adviser
- Leader in eligibility, feasibility discussion
- May interface with your entire project finance team as an integral part

like a deadline to motivate action, so even with my informed applicants, I like the 30-day program to put parameters around the workload. See Figure 8.2 for a look at how I structure the 30-day grant application process.

Prosperity's

30 DAYS TO A SUCCESSFUL GRANT PROPOSAL

A Start to Finish Process

* NOTE: Proposal may need more time to submit depending on method required by Agency and lead time needed to mail if hard copy required.

FIGURE 8.2

Thirty Days to a Successful Grant Proposal
Source: Created by Brandrenew.

TABLE 8.1 Project Team Roles

Project Owner		
(situated above the project manager in this hierarchy)		

Project Manager		
(situated above the expertise, developers, and financial aspects in this hierarchy)		

Specific Expertise	Proposal Developers	Financial
Professional engineer	Grant writer	CPA
Legal counsel	Copy editor	Legal services
Designer	Submit/deliver	Lender
Project developer	Content reviewers	Business plan consultant
Curriculum writer	Support contractors	Feasibility study writer
Vendors	Assembles required documentation	Market researcher
Builders/contractors		
Researchers		
Other implementers		

Table 8.1 demonstrates some of the roles you'll need to fill. The applicant is always at the top of the chart because this entire process is for their benefit, so regardless of how they fit in the team, they are ultimately the client. You will also see that there are three categories that project roles fall into: Specific Expertise, which varies by project and the GFO's requirements; Proposal Developers, which includes the tasks of turning all material into a final grant application and submittal; and Financial, which includes providers for materials related to financial documentation. A list of possible tasks or possible professionals you need to hire falls under each column.

Once you have a team, each member should be aware of his or her commitments. But if you are the owner, please don't assume they are. Use the project manager to do the following:

1. Create a schedule for everything, in advance of your kickoff call. Distribute it as an agenda.

2. Provide a schedule of the dates, review dates, and submission date. Realize all but the deadline are malleable; however, don't

allow just anybody to alter your schedule. Someone must own it and keep it on track.

3. Assign roles for each person and/or task. Everyone should have timelines.

4. Manage administrative tasks and correspondence volume in the team. Use polling to set calls, and use a conference call number for catch-up calls and a webinar program for group document review. Don't encourage people to copy in more individuals that necessary on each item they build. Too much follow-up is distracting.

5. Consider sending a weekly status e-mail to each team member and asking each to send a weekly status e-mail to the project manager indicating what is complete or yet in progress.

ALLOCATING YOUR TIME

My average grant application submission is an approximately 40-hour process. We've done many that take longer and some are shorter. Considering the majority, if I stacked all the time into one period, it would take about a business week's–worth of work. Now, that is just my work as a project manager. That doesn't include time for the applicant to gather documentation or other professionals to prepare materials. Plan this in advance as best you can. It will change, but you do not want to be completely caught off-guard by something you saved for the last day that requires a waiting period of two weeks.

The most sensible way to divide up your time is by importance of the application component. In Chapter 10 you will learn about responding to the merit criteria and how to possibly self-score your application. Some grants actually require that you include the score sheet with the application and provide documentation of the way each item you include meets the scoring criteria. This is actually quite handy and really helps with prioritization. The NOFA will indicate the factors for grant evaluation and will, in many cases, assign a weight to that factor. You could easily assume your level of work should correlate to the GFO's emphasis on each item it mentions.

TABLE 8.2 Sample Grant Application Time Allocation per Component

Component	Percentage of Time
Narrative	40
Forms/signatures	5
Supporting documents	5
Addendums	10
Financials	10
Identification numbers	5
Budget	20
Submission/confirmation	5
Total	100

Note: The information in this table counts review time for each aspect, including the narrative, in the total time allocated.

JUMP AHEAD

Jump to Chapter 10 to learn about how grant applications are scored.

For example, if one criterion is rated at 35 percent of total score and another at 10 percent, allocating your time resources to the section with the highest import to the GFO makes good sense. But, the GFO is not going to tell you how much emphasis it places on completing forms, signing all the documents, and obtaining your DUNS number. You know everything must be included, so you've got to fit that in, too. Table 8.2 gives an idea of how to allocate your time for the full grant package.

PREPARING THE APPLICATION

Finally, we are about to prepare the grant application. But, first I'd like you to confirm that you are ready to submit a quality proposal.

You do not have time to waste preparing a grant if your material and documentation are not even close to ready. I've designed the Prosperity Grant Planning Tool (see Appendix B) to help you make a sound go/no-go decision. Now that you're nearly finished reading this book, you'll likely take this assessment much earlier in the real-life process, but I mention it now so that you better understand why each question matters and how to answer them effectively. My clients must get a passing grade on the assessment or I am unable to assist them with grant funding. Keep a copy of this tool handy as you review future applications and modify some of the questions to fit your own industry or a specific GFO.

REVIEWING THE APPLICATION

You'll read some grant-writing manuals that encourage you to ask for numerous review rounds and offer your application up for scrutiny by scads of people inside and outside your organization. I think that is both unnecessary and impractical. Who has the time for multiple reviewers? What if they don't know the agency? What if they push it off-track?

I am not suggesting you skimp on quality grant reviewing and editing, but be really selective on this. I advocate two draft review periods in the 30-Day Grant Application Process you saw earlier, so I believe in the exercise. But, don't let this hold you up from submittal. You may have perfectly competent reviewers already among your team. You may have a colleague who offers to review the application and she has a certain expertise or experience with grant funding that you don't. Use as many reviewers as makes sense to improve the application without muddying the

> The very best reviewer is a representative at the GFO.

content with too many voices. Remember, the very best reviewer is a representative at the GFO. If that individual is willing to look over even a section of your application, you just gathered an excellent advantage. Even if he won't read your application but will let you describe your ideas and explain how you are responding to a certain set of criteria, that could pay dividends. Ask for this.

PERSPECTIVES ON PROSPERITY

> The prosperity of a people is proportionate to the number of hands and minds usefully employed.
>
> —*Samuel Johnson, English critic and poet*

Many hands may be required to ensure your path to prosperity, including the many hands you may employ in a project team. The way to avoid the too-many-cooks-in-the-kitchen scenario is to appoint a strong leader. This may be a grant writer, operating as an individual or as part of a consulting firm offering a package service replete with a total project team. Or, it may not include those individuals at all, and you, as the applicant, handle the role. Just as it takes only one successful grant to win the funding you desire, choose only the best hands on deck, too.

The most important aspects of this chapter concern these three key concepts:

1. The best grants are assembled by quality, well-thought-out teams.

2. Grant preparation requires someone to take a leadership role and direct the process, especially keeping everyone on schedule.

3. Using a structured process, such as a 30-day or even a 15-day plan, helps avoid confusion and overlooked details.

PART THREE

Application, Award, Afterward

CHAPTER NINE

Putting the Package Together

Narratives, budgets, and forms, oh my! Putting it all together takes work. You need a plan to package everything.

"You're going to love working with me," a new prospect gushed into the phone. "I had a professional writer prepare this beautifully crafted narrative—it's perfect. She actually did her thesis on my project."

"Sounds very thorough. What else do you have?" I countered.

"I have everything you need! Books and references and citations and clinical studies, and did I mention she has her MBA? The government will want to fund this project, no question about it."

Steering him back to the *how to*, I said: "We have a checklist of items required for this grant application. I'll get that to you as soon as we—" He cut me off with his enthusiasm.

"Oh, that's not necessary, with the time and money I spent getting this done your job will be a breeze. You'll even be happy taking the work on spec—it's a slam-dunk," he assured. "As a grant writer you *do* only get paid if we win, right?"

"Before we worry about that, I want to make sure you'll have everything needed since the application is due in a few weeks," I pursued.

We went on like that for a while and I even sent the prospect a partial checklist, not the grant-specific customized version (that goes only to paying clients), but a general checklist that covers most grants similar to what we'll be covering here. He didn't think he wanted to mess with all the items I suggested, however.

"You mean, I really have to get you all this stuff?"

Yes, you do. This is a further part of preparing (Step 4 of the Prosperity Process). This chapter is about creating output; we are ready to build a document that hopefully leads you to money.

Overall, this book is not like other grant-writing books that explain exactly how to write the perfect grant. I will not be redundant with those things in this section. While we are covering how to prepare an application, I maintain my spin on the strategic rather than the tactical. Again, there are a multitude of sources for those elements. This chapter breaks out the major components found in most grant applications and discusses how and when to use them. Not every piece will be required for every application, but just as there is no one federal or foundation there is no one exact set of components used in every case. Plan to address the components in this chapter and the application building team won't miss anything essential.

GRANT APPLICATION BASICS

Each year, I host a series of live training courses and update the accompanying course CD/mp3 download on the topic of the basics of grant applications. Since the full course is given over two 8-hour days, this section offers an abbreviated version. Here are the major components I find in grant applications:

- Narrative
- Forms, signatures, agreements
- Budget, including budget justification
- Supporting documentation
- Allowed addendums
- Financials
- Matching funds
- Score sheet, if allowed
- Identification and registration numbers

✒ Project or Idea

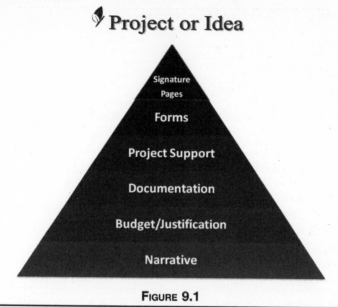

Signature
Pages

Forms

Project Support

Documentation

Budget/Justification

Narrative

FIGURE 9.1

Grant Application Pyramid
Source: Created by Kaitlin Ringer.

Figure 9.1 demonstrates the order of importance for each of these pieces. The narrative is the foundation, so it goes at the bottom and should be given the most attention. The forms are near the top and occupy the smallest segment. Each piece is essential; however, just like a pyramid, the lightest portions are at the top, held up by the steadiest at the bottom.

We'll cover each of these items in some detail in this chapter, breaking them out into further checklists and charts for your use. When taken as a whole, the easiest way to ensure that you never forget an item is to keep a checklist handy. Because many grant applications will have a table of contents (TOC) following the cover page, I've created a visual in that format as shown in Table 9.1.

Again, a great tip is to print out one of these for each major grant you work on and keep it in the file. I have a standard checklist that I use for all grant applications and then my team customizes it after combing through the funding notice for each application. The checklist we use stays in the file the entire time we are building the

TABLE 9.1 Grant Application Component

I. Title page
II. Table of contents
III. Project-specific forms
For example: standard forms such as SF 424, 424 C Form 990
IV. Certifications
Examples include: AD 1049 AD 1048 Form SF-LLL AD 1047 400-1 400-4 AD 3030
V. Legal organizational documents (*including any and all contracts*)
VI. Project summary (*including all the narrative pieces*)
VII. Self-evaluation score sheet (if needed)
VIII. Matching funds documentation
IX. Technical report
X. Financial documentation
XI. Budget and budget justification
XII. Addendums
XIII. Supporting documents

application and it's the last thing we look at before we submit. I recommend keeping guidance such as this so that when you get deep in details and editing you don't forget a simple form.

NARRATIVES

The word *narrative* covers a large category of possible documents you will create for your application. No one circumstance will require them all. While I've seen a few GFOs request simply "a narrative description of your project," that sort of thing would be for a fairly simplistic application. For major federal or foundations, I am broadly applying the term to the portion of the grant application you write compared to the portions of the application where you attach documentation, forms, and other supplements. The narrative portion of a grant application is not necessarily just one big document where you describe your project and mention its features and benefits. GFOs vary widely in narrative requirements. Length of narrative and format vary widely, too. For example, with highly technical grants, more photos and data are often required along with references to other research conducted on the topic. Grant requests for curriculum funding often emphasize proposed program design, the need for the program, and the facts on which that need is based.

I've never written a *statement of need* when requesting funds for construction, nor have I built a technical report when requesting dollars for a new youth program. Just like the jargon you use in your own industry, agencies tend to have their own terminology. It pays to learn that lingo and it's yet another reason I recommend becoming versed in a handful of GFOs. Sometimes, GFOs will consider one term synonymous with another, and sometime not, which can be frustrating. Always ask the GFO what the document is to specifically contain if the description does not make perfect sense to you.

Top Narrative Components Explained

Executive summary: Always best written last, this document, sometimes limited to as little as one page, is a standalone description of your funding request and the project's objectives, costs, and intended outcomes. It should be suitable for public distribution, so do not include sensitive material.

Abstract: An abstract is more like a snapshot of the project and application than an executive summary. Exec summaries lean toward PR while abstracts are more often used with technical and research grants. Again, this is a short document.

Project description: A project description usually includes the longest page length in the application packet. Be prepared to pull out the stops here in terms of everything you need to make your case and document it. Should the description length be 20 pages or more (and some will number into 100 pages or more), include a short table of contents (TOC) at the beginning.

Statement of need: The need statement and position statement have similarities. I've seen these terms used interchangeably, but I don't believe they are synonyms. This statement is literally to inform the GFO why its dollars are needed to support the project. Often used in foundation grants and in the health and research fields, this document can be written to evoke an emotional response in the reader. The reviewers should read this and come away believing their money will make an important impact, so providing supporting resources to point up the magnitude of the problem to be addressed is essential.

Statement of position: When a NOFA requests this document, reviewers look to learn your take, position, or impression on the issue your project is to solve. Are you taking a stance with the project? If so, describe it and explain why the GFO should also take that stance by funding it.

Work plan: This document is the place to provide detail on your ability to accomplish the work in an organized, timely manner. You will often include timelines, milestones, and job roles for those involved. Commonly, the GFO will ask you to address go/no-go points, meaning that you should describe a milestone to be reached and what happens if it is not, or if the timing is delayed. Grants of all types require some kind of work plan. In my experience, the NOFA details specifics to include, so read that carefully.

Project management plan: Here's another document that may overlap; there could be similarities between this and the work plan. Here highlight intended job roles and team players for the project and their expertise. You should provide reasons why individuals on the team are suited to the project and how many hours a week or month they will work and if they will be onsite or contracted. Project management plans are commonly requested when the grant period is two years or longer, so you should write a plan for each year.

Technical report: Grants for construction and implementation of equipment often require this component. You'll be asked to address topics such as an equipment description, why the equipment was chosen, who will install it, and a timeline for installation. Technical reports may include a discussion of external factors potentially affecting the project (such as the condition of the existing site, environmental factors present, and permitting required).

Letter of intent: If the agency required a letter of intent (LOI), you must do it, unless it specifies it as optional. Usually, this is simply a statement with a short project description (a couple of paragraphs) indicating that you intend to apply. Federal agencies often request these in advance of the application due date and will not accept grant applications that did not file an LOI in time. You may receive a tracking number or an ID to include with your full grant application as a response from your successfully received LOI.

Concept paper: Concept papers and LOIs go together. Again, if one is required prior to the application deadline, turn it in or risk being disqualified for a full application. Usually, the GFO gives guidelines for the concept paper, including page length and any required addendums. It's a short document, likely less than 10 pages allowed. Be advised that it's also fairly common that the GFO uses the concept paper to shrink its pool of full applications. Check the NOFA to see if full applications following concept papers are by invitation only.

Tips for Narratives

Recall the prospect from the chapter opener, the one with the beautiful narrative? Well, he opted not to work with me—no surprise there. I did raise a brow, however, when six months later a package arrived from him. I opened it and found what appeared to be his grant application, a rejection letter from the GFO, and a note requesting that I call him to discuss my services. The note added, "I get it; you do have to send them what they ask for."

Yes, you do.

The problem with the prospect's application was that he spent all his time polishing up the piece he loved—that beautifully written narrative. It *was* nicely done. But, it was not what the grant guidelines requested. Being that he was applying for a technical grant, he was to show third-party reviews and he supplied only his own research. There was a specific report to complete addressing the technical material—he simply made a note where the report was to be inserted and directed the reviewer back to his beautiful narrative. All the technical details required for the report were included there, but the reviewer is not going to look elsewhere when she is expecting a specific report. Even the signature pages required were left blank. Instead, he provided a coversheet detailing his excellent resume and noted that if in fact the agency offered him the grant, he would sign the forms then. I'd seen some bull-headed people in the past, but this prospect was at the top 1 percent of that club. Reaching for the denial letter, I read that his application was rejected solely on the basis of incompleteness. Sadly, his beautiful narrative had never been read because his incomplete application package did not meet the minimum of requested documentation. That, coupled with his attitude, basically screamed at the agency: "I, personally, am above the guidelines that all those other applicants have to adhere to!"

No, you're not.

The most common reason why I see grant applications denied is because they are incomplete.

Here are some tips to improve your narratives:

- Start with the key points and emphasize them repeatedly. Don't get to the middle before mentioning the big value of the project or the way it meets the GFO's objectives. That always goes first.

- Include website URLs for documentation, but not for reference. Include the data directly in the document. Many GFOs will be kind enough to tell you that they will not look at websites; most don't and won't. If it matters, write about it; don't just cite it.

- Follow the guidelines, including the style, page limit, font size, margin width, and any other seemingly mundane requests of the grant agency. This is an easy way to look professional or an easy way to appear like an amateur.

- Do not include extra sections not required, even if you believe it would be nice to add them. It's a waste of time and a distraction to the reviewer.

- If the narrative portion consists only of a project summary, don't bother crafting a separate statement of need. Build the value for the project into the description requested. The reviewer has plenty of these to score and won't hunt for your main points.

- Use images, charts, and graphs in good balance with solid, well-structured explanatory text.

- It should go without saying: Do not use old data (more than three years old) unless your point is to say that the latest data available is old, and that somehow validates your work (it certainly might!).

- Write seriously, unless there is a very good reason to be more creative. I have seen proposals with very hokey language and wordy, cheesy descriptions of how special the project is for which they are requesting funds. It's a turnoff and it makes you appear unprofessional, or worse, not legitimate.

Do not include extra sections not required, even if you believe it would be nice to add them. It's a waste of time and a distraction to the reviewer.

- Write as though you are explaining the project to your mom, or the uninformed, while still being technically accurate. Break down the project.

- Do not write as though it's all about you. Cover the benefits to many, the benefits to the agency, the way the project meets and furthers its objectives. That you benefit from this work is obvious if you are receiving funds.

The moral of this story is simple, but extremely important: Don't focus only on the big pie—the narrative components—and neglect the other documentation. The usual reason why I see grant applications denied is because they are incomplete—by the GFO's standards and not necessarily the applicant's. Submitting an incomplete application is nothing more than an easy route to File 13 (also known as the trashcan!). Let's look at other items you may need to include.

FORMS AND SIGNATURES

When applying for grant funding, the paper trail is long and your arm may tire from signing your name. Some wholly online submissions require no signatures at all, simply a checked box that indicates you agree to the terms, but that option is still the exceptional case and not the rule. The nature of forms required often surprises my clients. See the list of *standard forms* (SFs) later in this chapter for a sampling of commonly required forms.

For any given application, you may sign that you:

- Are not delinquent on any federal debts
- Have not recently been convicted of a felony
- Have not recently won an award for the same grant

In other cases, by signing a form, you may have to certify:

- Your status as a lobbyist
- Whether you or a family member are employed by the GFO or its affiliate
- That you are not currently involved in a lawsuit
- That you will use vendors and contractors meeting certain wage standards

The preceding list of examples is short, but the possible topics on which you may have to signify, certify, or verify is nearly exhaustive.

Outside of the aforementioned, there is not much to say about forms and signature pages save the following points:

1. Read them carefully and be certain you understand the implications. Should you find that you do not agree with or cannot comply with something stated on a form or in the required signature document, it may be that you have to forgo the application. You are unlikely to change those documents, especially the SFs required for federal grants. Convincing the GFO to change its in-house signature document or agreement is also a longshot, but I've seen it occur. Good luck with that one.

2. Regarding forms, be sure to complete them.

3. SFs are occasionally updated; obtain the most current version for each grant. Many are in PDF format and can be downloaded at the OPM.gov website: http://www.opm.gov/forms/standard-forms/.

   Commonly Used Standard Forms:
   - SF-424
   - SF-424A
   - SF-424C
   - SF-242D

- SF-LLL
- RD 400-4
- RD-1940
- AD-1047
- AD-3030

BUDGET AND JUSTIFICATION

In Chapter 8, we discussed how to build a team and whether you needed an actual grant writing professional to successfully win grants. As you learned, I don't believe it is necessary to hire a grant professional in every case. Budgets and budget justifications are one area where it pays to contract professional grant-oriented assistance. If you have a simple grant application requesting only that you include a budget, and it provides no guidelines or template, by all means complete that yourself.

However, in the case of multiyear grant requests or large federal opportunities, consider hiring an experienced professional skilled at budgeting for the grant world. Grant application budgets aren't necessarily the same as the type of budget you'd put together for your business. They often require their own format, much of which seems redundant to applicants. The budget template shown in Figure 9.2 is from an actual grant program I've worked with several times, the USDA Value Added Producer Grant. We also discussed this grant when I reviewed the *notice of funding* earlier in this book.

Once you've prepared the budget, you may also have to complete the GFO's budget justification template. This type of document requires that you attach certain measurable points to each line item in your budget. Further, you may have to assign a timeline for completion of each item and, further still, an individual who will do the work. I am often asked what minimum cost should be included in the budget. The GFO will often supply that minimum; I see costs for over $1,000 pretty regularly.

Figure 9.3 shows the budget justification template from the value-added grant that accompanies the budget template.

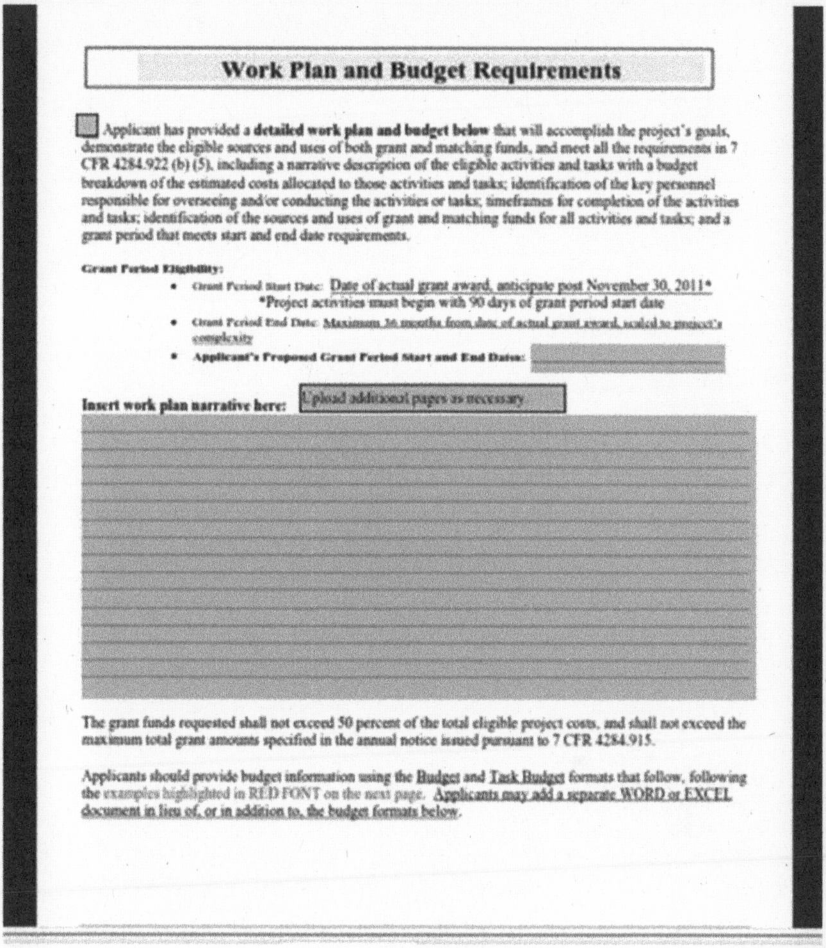

Work Plan and Budget Requirements

☐ Applicant has provided a **detailed work plan and budget below** that will accomplish the project's goals, demonstrate the eligible sources and uses of both grant and matching funds, and meet all the requirements in 7 CFR 4284.922 (b) (5), including a narrative description of the eligible activities and tasks with a budget breakdown of the estimated costs allocated to those activities and tasks; identification of the key personnel responsible for overseeing and/or conducting the activities or tasks; timeframes for completion of the activities and tasks; identification of the sources and uses of grant and matching funds for all activities and tasks; and a grant period that meets start and end date requirements.

Grant Period Eligibility:

- Grant Period Start Date: Date of actual grant award, anticipate post November 30, 2011*
  *Project activities must begin with 90 days of grant period start date
- Grant Period End Date: Maximum 36 months from date of actual grant award, scaled to project's complexity
- **Applicant's Proposed Grant Period Start and End Dates:**

Insert work plan narrative here: Upload additional pages as necessary

The grant funds requested shall not exceed 50 percent of the total eligible project costs, and shall not exceed the maximum total grant amounts specified in the annual notice issued pursuant to 7 CFR 4284.915.

Applicants should provide budget information using the Budget and Task Budget formats that follow, following the examples highlighted in RED FONT on the next page. Applicants may add a separate WORD or EXCEL document in lieu of, or in addition to, the budget formats below.

FIGURE 9.2

Sample Budget Template

Source: USDA Valued-Added Producer Grant program http://www.rurdev.usda.gov/BCP_VAPG.html.

Even if a budget justification template is not required, always describe why budget items are needed, somewhere in the narrative. One sensible place to provide the information is where you address project costs.

There are ways to improve budgets—the biggest one is simply checking over them for accuracy. Here are a few problems that can

FIRST: In the **Budget Format**, identify *each main activity* in your project budget (i.e. For P: hire consultant to conduct feasibility study, marketing plan and/or business plan. For WC: conduct marketing campaign, purchase inventory supplies, contract for value-added processing etc.).

Budget Format – list each main activity

Activity #	Task Name and Description	Start Date	End Date	Federal VAPG Funds	Cash Matching Funds	In-Kind Matching Funds	Total Project Costs
Example	*Perform Market Research* Description: Identify potential customers, provide samples to prospective customers, determine price points and specifications, identify distribution channels, develop marketing plan. Name of Contractor, Vendor, or Staff who will be Paid for this task: EcoFuel Marketing, Inc.	10/1/2011	3/1/2012	$18,000	$9,000 from applicant	$9,000 from EcoFuel Marketing, Inc. for pro bono time on Example Activity	$36,000
1				$	$	$	$
2							
3							
4							
5							
6							
7							
8							
9							
	TOTAL PROJECT			$	$	$	$

FIGURE 9.2

(Continued)

be prevented or easily fixed:

- Incorrectly identifying the applicant and GFO and matching portions
- Using more than the allowed percent of in-kind, leveraged, or other matching funds

AND THEN: In the **Task Budget Format**, provide detailed information for *each task* that will be completed for *each main activity* listed above. [Upload additional pages as necessary]

Example Task Budget – **Perform Market Research**

Budget Item	VAPG Funds	Total Matching Funds	Total Cost
Personnel	$	$	$
Fringe Benefits	$	$	$
Travel	$ 2,000	$	$ 2,000
Office Equipment	$	$	$
Supplies	$	$	$
Contractual	$16,000	$18,000	$34,000
Other	$	$	$
Other	$	$	$
Other	$	$	$
Other	$	$	$
TOTAL	$18,000	$18,000	$36,000

Provide explanation/clarification of the basis for the above budget figures:
This task requires significant interaction with potential customers including customer site visits, product demonstrations, surveys and specification analysis, conference attendance by consultant, and research and analyses of distribution channels. Travel estimates for this task include one consultant airfare for $750 roundtrip to Boston, MA to attend the Northeast Regional Bio-fuels Conference in November 2011; and 2,500 car miles at $0.50 per mile or $1,250 for all other market research travel by consultant. Consultant fees derive from 100 days labor at $340 per day, inclusive of costs for phone, postage, and supplies.

Task Budget for Activity 1 –

Budget Item	VAPG Funds	Total Matching Funds	Total Cost
Personnel	$	$	$
Fringe Benefits	$	$	$
Travel	$	$	$
Office Equipment	$	$	$
Supplies	$	$	$
Contractual	$	$	$
Other	$	$	$
Other	$	$	$
Other	$	$	$
Other	$	$	$
TOTAL	$	$	$

Provide explanation/clarification of the basis for the above budget figures:

FIGURE 9.2

(Continued)

- Listing less than the required percent of matching funds
- Not providing the required budget detail for each year funds are requested
- Budgets that don't add up
- Budgets that look canned or made up

Task	Start Date	End Date	Budget Federal	Cash	In-Kind	Total
Producer meetings Responsible Staff:						
Establish product line Responsible Staff:						
Packaging bidding Responsible Staff:						
Distribution negotiations Responsible Staff:						
Issue "want list" Responsible Staff:						
Establish packaging suppliers Responsible Staff						
Review distribution agreement Responsible Staff						
Product line brochure Responsible Staff						
Confirm sales Responsible Staff						
Conduct follow-up with producers Responsible Staff						
Procurement of packaging material Responsible Staff						
Establish distribution agreement Responsible Staff						
Hire Processing Kitchen manager Responsible Staff						
Establish reports Responsible Staff						
Purchase required supplies, product Responsible Staff						
Generate reports Responsible Staff						
Hire 1 part-time employee Responsible Staff						
Begin processing Responsible Staff						
Confirm commitments Responsible Staff						
Begin distribution Responsible Staff						
Hire 3 part-time employees Responsible Staff						
Purchase required supplies, product Responsible Staff						
Generate reports Responsible Staff						
Continue sales Responsible Staff						
Continue distribution Responsible Staff						
Overhead expenses Responsible Staff						
Total Cost of Project						

FIGURE 9.3

Sample Budget Justification Template

Source: USDA Valued-Added Producer Grant program http://www.rurdev.usda.gov/
BCP_VAPG.htm.

SUPPORTING DOCUMENTATION

If you thought a 100-page narrative was a lot of material to assemble, that's nothing compared to the potential volume of these next two categories. I've submitted grants of 500, 600, even 700 pages. While the narrative was long, much of the size was from additional documentation such as I will list here. Take heart; while the volume can be high, many of these items require time to obtain, but not time to create, making them easier than the narrative. Your biggest challenge may be formatting them to attach properly online, or worse yet, not burning out three industrial-size copiers building a paper submission. And there's the shipping cost for the resulting behemoth.

Supporting documentation validates your case with the GFO. It should go without saying: Don't contribute anything that doesn't sing your project's praises. Make certain everything looks great; don't include fuzzy images that indicate nothing discernible or charts so large they run off the page. If possible, format your documents similarly.

It seems as though everyone loves support letters but me. Politicians love support letters, local economic development professionals love support letters, city leaders love support letters, and applicants love accumulating support letters. I don't care much for support letters unless the agency specifically tells you they want a support letter. I'm a less-is-more preparer when it comes to grants—give the agency what it needs and be done. One thing that the agency does not need to make a decision on your application is a form letter. Should you read other grant-writing books, you will find I differ from peers. Authors of other grant-writing books I've reviewed advocate an abundance of support letters. One fellow grant writer encourages applicants to obtain a support letter from every Congressional representative in their area for every grant application. Another compares support letters to personal recommendations, saying you can never have too many. I do not like support letters that are sent to the GFO separate from your application package. How will you ever know if that one letter, floating in a sea of envelopes in a federal mailroom, will ever make it to your application file? You don't. I just don't see the value. As you'll see in

Chapter 10, there are many better ways to grease the skids and improve your chances of winning a grant.

If the GFO requires a letter or some kind of endorsement, do not fail to obtain it *in a timely fashion*—specifically, by the due date. Or, if the agency mentions that a support letter is optional, please find the best letter you can obtain that includes real specifics about your project.

Checklist of Supporting Documentation:
- Research
- Images, drawings, charts
- Bios and resumes
- Related works by the applicant
- Related grants funded by GFO
- Support letters

Don't overlook the value of the nice-to-add items if the NOFA mentions them as optional. I read *optional* to mean one of two things:

1. You will receive extra points for this item when they score your application (even if they don't say so in the NOFA).

2. You should include it because it's something the GFO deems important, even if they didn't require it, and you might lose points if it's not in there (even if they don't mention that fact).

ADDENDUMS

Addendums and supporting documentation certainly overlap. One item here could easily be in another list and vice versa. I categorize them differently based on what is required. Here are some items I commonly see requested in addendums:

- Technical reports
- Review by a third party

- Bank letters showing funds available
- Commitment from buyers and suppliers
- Environmental reviews
- Clearance letters from the government agencies
- Business plans
- Calculations or formulas
- Surveys conducted

FINANCIALS

Your financial position matters to the GFO. Depending on the size of the grant request and the agency, you may be supplying just cursory information about your or your organization's finances, or it may be quite detailed. Many entrepreneurs feel this type of material is invasive. If that is the case, the grant program may not be for you. It is unlikely the GFO will waive a requirement for financial documentation. I also don't recommend sending any financials not required.

Common items for inclusion are:

- State and federal income tax returns (1 to 3 years)
- Letters from a CPA or other third-party financial professional, verifying accuracy of financials
- Annual report
- Sales or other income projections (for 1 to 5 years)
- Balance sheets
- Income statements
- Property tax statements
- A listing of liens from your creditors

Note that you're not off the hook just because you are a startup with limited documentation. If you have no previous income tax returns, for example, you may have to supply personal financials. Also, when partnering, it's entirely possible that each partner must supply financial documentation.

MATCHING FUNDS DOCUMENTATION

In Part One of this book, I busted two prevailing myths about grant funding. Number One: it is a myth that grants are 'free money' because there is always a cost associated with the grant funding process. Number Two: it is a myth to expect grant programs to cover the cost of everything involved in a project because most grants require matching funds. Here we'll further discuss the meaning of matching funds and how to meet a matching funds requirement. Basically, matching funds are the proof of other resources available to cover costs exceeding the grant request. This documentation is referred to as the *match*. In the case of matching dollars, we simply call it *matching funds*. Some GFOs will refer to the match as the *leveraged funds*; however, I use that term separately (see ahead).

Depending on what is required in the NOFA, you may have options when it comes to documenting your match. There are two types of matching resources: cash or in-kind. Within these two broad categories are sub-options. For example, if a cash match is required you could demonstrate that by providing a current bank statement or even a letter from your bank verifying the statement. A cash match can also be demonstrated by a line of credit, a loan taken out for the project, or funds provided from an investor or partner. It is possible that another grant can be used as the match. In-kind contributions are resources other than cash brought to the project. Options for these may include work already completed with a particular value to the project, land, equipment, or other hard assets donated, or labor and expertise donated by qualified providers. Leveraged funds are a combination of the above, as grant agencies may want to see leverage from a variety of other organizations to help offset costs to the applicant and demonstrate a broad commitment to the applicant's project.

GRANTS GURU GLOSSARY

Matching funds: Documentation of the funds or other resources available to the grant applicant to cover project costs exceeding the grant request are referred to as the *match*.

IDENTIFICATION AND REGISTRATION NUMBERS

Account numbers abound for grant applications. Table 9.2 lists several of the commonly required IDs or registration numbers you may have to obtain. Fortunately, the NOFA will indicate what is required; do not forget to look for these when you study the guidelines. Even if you are a sole proprietor and file your taxes under your Social Security number (SSN), you may need to obtain a *data universal numbering system* (DUNS) number. Early in the application process, determine what is required. If you don't have the required numbers, or if they have not been updated lately, begin applying for these immediately; they can take several days to a couple of weeks to obtain.

Note that you will use each of the items in Table 9.2 repeatedly during the process and repeatedly if you apply for multiple grants. Keep them handy and keep them up-to-date. The same goes for any certifications and licenses you hold that require renewal.

PERSPECTIVES ON PROSPERITY

Industry is the soul of business and the keystone of prosperity.
—*Charles Dickens*

This chapter and this part of the book are all about being industrious in pursuit of grant funding as they are the manufacturing centers of the process, Step 4: Prepare. Most grant applications will require most of the nine primary components covered in detail in the chapter. Be on the lookout for each of these.

TABLE 9.2 Commonly Required Registration and Account Numbers

Registration Name	Registration Acronym	Description	Website
System for Award Management	SAM	The system where you register in order to get a Commercial and Governmental Entity (CAGE) code.	https://www.sam.gov/portal/public/SAM/
Tax Identification Number	TIN	A TIN is an identifying number used for tax purposes in the United States that is reported on grant applications.	https://irs-tax-id.com/?gclid=CO26muTtmLcCFYU-Mgod2HwAag
Employer Identification Number	EIN	The Employer Identification Number is commonly used by employers for the purpose of reporting taxes on grant applications.	https://irs-ein-number.com/?gclid=CM2Dydrum LcCFVN0MgodojlAAg
Data Universal Numbering System	DUNS	The DUNS number is a nine-digit number, issued by Dun and Bradstreet (D&B), assigned to each business location in the D&B database, having a unique, separate, and distinct operation for the purpose of identifying them.	http://www.dnb.com/
Social Security Number	SSN	A Social Security number (SSN) is a nine-digit number issued to U.S. citizens under Section 205(c)(2) of the Social Security Act. This number is sometimes needed in grant applications to prove citizenship.	
Grant Proposal ID		A number assigned by GFO during the application process, possibly upon receipt of a concept paper or LOI.	This is provided by the GFO, if required.

■ 168 ■

There comes a point where you simply have to get working. No amount of strategizing builds an application. Given you now know that even the most basic federal grant will take you a good 40 hours to complete, you can certainly understand the labor and time involved in completing a solid package. Grants are laborious and boring work much of the time. One positive is that there is always a timeframe on the workload. For all the evenings, late nights, early mornings, and weekends I've spent at my desk trying to make a budget add up or piece together a narrative from the varying perspectives of five different engineers, I could always say to myself: "I'd rather be out drinking wine with my girlfriends tonight, but this will be turned in quite soon." I've used impending deadlines as motivation and many other unique self-promises to stay at my desk and see some really tough applications through. When you're work- ing for yourself, that's what you do. You might question if it's worth it, but when you know it must be done, you as an entrepreneur won't question the fact and will find a way to stick it out.

Perseverance is one reason I think small-business owners are a fit for grant funding. Crafting a winning grant application may not allow you to quit at 5 P.M. every night, but you're already used to that.

CHAPTER TEN

Scoring Your Application

> You've worked so hard completing this application, but now it's out of your hands. It's time to see how you score.

"What am I evaluated on?"

"Is there a way to find out who is reviewing my grant?"

"What qualifies someone to review grants?"

"Are there certain standards by which all grants are measured?"

"Does the notice actually say how I will be scored?"

"Can I score myself? Against what baseline?"

Questions and concerns flood applicants' minds at this point in the process. They wake up worrying about something and call me in the middle of the night! Grant seekers get self-conscious not long before the submission deadline and it's no wonder: They've been working really hard to get the package together in an attractive, sensible format that follows the guidelines. It's been a big job. Invariably, about this time, my clients begin to turn from focusing on themselves to considering how the grant agency will see their application package. This transition is really important both for obtaining a realistic point of view on an application's success chances and for identifying holes that you still have time to improve.

For every new prospect I consult with I start by picturing their project in terms of the big outcome they want to achieve. Then, I move to the tactics that will take them to that goal, and finally dissect it through the lens of a grant agency score sheet. It's almost as though I put on special glasses allowing me to see only one thing, and that thing is the grid of the GFO's score sheet.

This chapter discusses the final stages of Step 4 and covers three major topics:

1. A discussion showing the means by which grants are evaluated

2. An example of grant scoring from my time at a grant agency where I've completed successful applications

3. Some of my best grant submission tips

EVALUATING A GRANT PROPOSAL

Merit criteria review sounds like the worst performance evaluation ever. It *is* a tough performance review, and this time it's for money. Potentially, the merit criteria stand between you and a big check. What does this term mean?

GRANTS GURU GLOSSARY

Merit criteria: This is the GFO's set of factors upon which your grant is measured for quality, completeness, and ultimately funding acceptability.

Simply put, merit criteria, or *grant evaluation score* or *evaluation metrics*, is the GFO's set of factors upon which your grant is measured for quality, completeness, and ultimately funding.

Merit criteria, or *grant evaluation score* or *evaluation metrics*, is simply the GFO's set of factors upon which your grant is measured for quality, completeness, and ultimately funding. Not all GFOs use the term *merit criteria*, but I find it common enough, and potentially confusing enough to share grant-speak here.

There is absolutely no one set of grant evaluation criteria that make grant scoring standard—far from it. Your GFO will include the criteria that matter to its organization. Sometimes these evaluation criteria are not written in industry-standard language. You may be asked to submit supporting material that is outside of the norm of accepted standards in industry. This really frustrates entrepreneurs and often their vendors. For example, I have worked with a number of CPAs who have told me that the typical statements they prepare are usually geared toward the needs of the financial services industry, as their clients often use these to help them obtain a loan. When preparing these for grant applications, CPAs often indicate that required financials seem too invasive compared to what lenders require; at other times, the required material seems to lack the level of detail that will pass the scrutiny of an industry professional.

Why there is no standard, I don't know. What I can tell you is that each grant program is built to accomplish an objective; legislators appropriate dollars that become federal initiatives just as a foundation's board of directors creates a grant program to further their mission through a specific funding opportunity. When staff write the programs, those crafters are attempting to build a program where they can assign a set of eligible applicants with a score that is as objective as possible. You cannot change the criteria, at least not at this point (recall you may be able to influence how programs are written at the federal level through the comment period process). The only course of action is to determine how to make your application score as high as possible.

The list that follows offers some of the typical criteria used to evaluate grant applications. Most NOFAs will list these, so be on the hunt for them. There may also be templates from the agency that can describe the merit criteria or even an additional guidance document where criteria are further delineated.

Common Merit Criteria:
- Were the milestones reached?
- Were the timelines realistic?
- Were outcomes measurable?
- How is the overall completeness?
- Are objectives reasonable?

- How does the budget justification stack up?
- Does the applicant appear ready?
- Is the quality and expertise of the project team demonstrated?

Never fail to respond to a listed merit criterion if a score is associated with it. Even if you don't think your project fits into that criterion, find a way to address it.

For each area of evaluation the agency deems important, it will assign it a value. Usually, the NOFA will indicate how much weight, often expressed as a percentage of total possible score, is given to each category. This is open to interpretation.

Objective and Subjective Grant Evaluation

Here's a thought that bothers some applicants: The grant applications you've worked so hard to prepare will in all or in part be evaluated on a completely subjective basis.

You read that correctly: The grant will be reviewed by a real human being, or worse yet, a committee of them, or worse still, a committee of them spread out across different time zones and continents and with completely different backgrounds. Further, your grant may be reviewed by peers, that is, professionals in the industry, or solely by GFO staff, who may have never been in the industry. Retired executives, trade association representatives, or even fulltime for-hire grant writers may all be among your reviewers. If these individuals are not agency staff, they may volunteer, be paid a salary, or simply receive a small stipend for evaluating your application. There is nothing about the process of grant review that resembles an objective standard. If you were picturing your application going in one side of a computer and coming out the other with an objectively generated score, you're wrong. So, how do you contend with all

> The grant applications you've worked so hard to prepare will in all or in part be evaluated on a completely subjective basis.

these opportunities for discrepancy? You prepare by knowing what you can and cannot impact.

Objective Scoring Items.   These are the items for which the GFO can basically check the box and confirm that you have completed. Once they are all accounted for, realize they total up to one very important factor—a complete application. Remember, a common reason for grant rejection is an incomplete application package. These little items are all part of a complete application. Never overlook the small stuff with grant funding:

- Forms, signatures

- Account numbers, ID numbers, reference numbers

- Financials (though these walk the line between objective and subjective because a professional may evaluate your projections and question their merits, thus questioning the project in general)

Subjective Scoring Items.   In my view, the subjective scoring items are most of the things the GFO includes in its merit criteria. The GFO has asked for these specifically. Here's the catch: Even if you respond to each criterion it still doesn't ensure a perfect score. While you may feel as though you responded thoroughly, the reviewers may not. While you may feel as though your included research is excellent, the reviewers may not think it's good enough. This can be frustrating, but there are ways to improve your subjective evaluation scores. First, always ask questions. Second, if they are not accepting direct correspondence, check to see if there is a question-and-answer document you can review. Third, research the previous years' winners in the same program. If you can find a project similar to yours, read whatever you can about that project.

SCORING POINTS

Once you've identified the criteria that you are responsible for meeting, it's time to total them up and decide how well you meet those expectations. You have to determine whether you are on the track to funding or to failure. In order to do that, you should self-score your application.

Building Your Own (Probable) Score

Crafting your own potential score is fairly easy to do. First, total the number of merit categories you can find in the NOFA or grant guidance documents. Then, total the possible points or percentages assigned to each category. Following that, begin to evaluate your application for each section critically. Answer the following questions:

- Are you extremely strong in any one area?
- Does your documentation or research stand out particularly well?
- Compared to the merit criteria, did your materials read as though the GFO wrote the guidelines just for you?

So, what did you find out?

Here's what I do. If the application is really strong in any one area, score it in the 80–90 percent range for the total points. For example, if the GFO assigned those criteria 35 points, give yourself 80 to 90 percent of 35, or 28–31.5 points.

Now, evaluate where your application is weaker. No application is ever perfect, so don't kid yourself. This is not the time to look at how convincing you'll try to be to the GFO; it's the time to look for holes.

Answer these questions:

- Is there anything missing—perhaps something you're waiting on and are unsure you can obtain?

  If something is completely missing, score yourself harshly there, frankly awarding zero points for that category.

- What if you find something that you know is decent, but not completely perfect?

Go ahead and score that reasonably low to medium, say 40 to 60 percent of total points available.

Next, add each of these up and give yourself a total. But wait—the score is not done yet.

There's an additional piece: Add or subtract from the total number you just tallied based upon the weight the agency puts on each category. For example, if you have five criteria and they are given percentages of 30, 35, 25, 5, and 5, respectively, prioritize your scores for each based on the highest-weighted categories receiving more emphasis. So, in this case, 30 percent of your total score is based 30 percent on the first criterion, 35 percent upon the second, and so on. You'll be adjusting your number a few points in either direction based on how well you think you're doing in comparison to what the GFO cares about most.

Now, what's your number?

- How well did you do?
- Out of 100, are you above 80 percent or below 60 percent?

Here's where I lack science because grant evaluation is subjective. I cannot definitively say that if you score an 80 percent in your view, you will score an 80 percent in the agency's view. We do not know about the size of the application pool or the quality of peer applications. We also do not know if the GFO has an internal priority not published or at least not clearly stated in the NOFA (that happens). But, if you take time to critically evaluate your application, you'll accomplish two things:

1. You'll recognize areas for improvement before submission.
2. You'll realize that if you cannot improve those lower-scoring areas, then you will simply have to live with the results.

Ultimately, this process helps you temper expectations downward or upward, depending on your best possible self-assessment.

Self-Evaluation Score

There is the possibility you'll be saved from estimating all these categories; a score sheet in the template or guidance document accompanies some applications. The GFO may even require you to include this sheet as documentation. These are often referred to as *self-evaluation score sheets*, and are quite handy.

Note that within a single given grant notice, there may be criteria you are not required to meet. This is because grant programs are often broad, allowing several different kinds of projects or applicants to apply and compete for the same pool of funds. So, varying documentation is required for different merits or for different applicants or eligible projects. See the score sheet in Figure 10.1, for example. In this program, both renewable energy and energy efficiency applicants may apply. The documentation and technical merit required for each are unique. Thus, if you are applying for an efficiency project, you need not meet the renewables requirements. Take note of these possible variances, and ask the agency if you are unsure.

As you examine the self-evaluation score sheet in Figure 10.1, take notice of the following things:

- The points do not total 100.
- Any one applicant simply does not meet the eligibility for all points.
- Applicants are not required to meet all items.
- Varying types of applicants or projects are scored on the same sheet.
- Some of the items are clearly objective; others are clearly not.

The following is a list of final tips for grant scoring:

- If no score sheet is included in the application package, this is yet another reason to
  - Read the NOFA thoroughly and repeatedly.
  - Ask the GFO questions about its evaluation criteria.

SCORING POINTS

Rural Energy for America Program
Evaluation Criteria Scoring Guideline
Per April 14, 2011 Interim Rule - 4280.117 (c)

Name of Applicant: APPLICANT

Type of Technology: Grain Dryer Replacement, Energy Efficiency Project

Funding Request: GRANT AMOUNT

Final Grant Score (sum of Categories 1-9):

(1) Quantity of Energy Replaced, Produced, or Saved.
Points may only be awarded for one category (A, B, C or D).

(i) Energy Replacement
If the proposed renewable energy system is <u>intended primarily for self use</u> by the agricultural producer or rural small business, and will provide energy replacement of:

	Points
Greater than 0 but equal to or less than 25%, **award 5 points.**	
Greater than 25%, but equal to or less than 50%, **award 10 points.**	
Greater than 50%, **award 15 points.**	
Determine energy replacement by dividing the estimated quantity of renewable energy to be generated over a 12 month period by the estimated quantity of energy consumed over the same 12 month period during the previous year by the applicable energy application. The estimated quantities of energy must be converted to British thermal units (BTU's), Watts, or similar energy equivalents to facilitate scoring. If the estimated energy produced equals more than 150% of the energy requirements of the applicable process(es), score the project as an energy generation project.	n/a

Documentation in the file to substantiate the score for this category.

or

(ii) Energy Savings (include additional 5 points if applicable)

(1) If the estimated energy expected to be saved by the installation of the energy efficiency improvements will be from:

	Points
20% up to but not including 30%, **award 5 points.**	
30% up to but not including 35%, **award 10 points.**	
35% or greater, **award 15 points.**	
Energy savings will be determined by the projections in an energy assessment or audit. If capacity changes, savings should be pro-rated to similar size of existing equipment/facility.	

(2) Additional points.

	Points
If the project has total eligible project costs of $50,000 or less AND opts to obtain a professional energy audit, **award an additional 5 points.**	n/a

Documentation in the file to substantiate the score for this category.
The independent energy audit conducted by Purdue University indicates that the percent of energy saved is %.

or

(iii) Energy Generation

	Points
If the proposed renewable energy system is intended primarily for production of energy for sale, **award 10 points.**	n/a

Documentation in the file to substantiate the score for this category.

or

FIGURE 10.1

Sample Score Sheet Used with Grant Application to Be Scored by the Applicant

Source: USDA's Rural Energy for America Program (REAP), http://www.rurdev.usda.gov/ORreap_renew_grants.html.

SCORING YOUR APPLICATION

(iv) Flexible Fuel Pump(s)

If the proposed project is for one or more flexible fuel pumps, points will be awarded based on the overall percentage of proposed flexible fuel pumps to the applicant's total retail pump inventory at the facility. If the proposed flexible fuel pump percentage is:

	Points
5% or below, **award 5 points.**	
Above 5% and up to but not including 10%, **award 10 points.**	
10% or greater, **award 15 points.**	n/a
The percentage of proposed flexible fuel pumps shall be calculated using the following equation: **Equation: FFP% = (FFPx/TP) x 100** FFP% = Proposed flexible fuel pump(s) percentage. FFPx = Number of proposed flexible fuel pumps to be installed at applicants facility. TP = Number of proposed pumps to be installed plus the number of pumps installed and operating at the facility.	

Documentation in the file to substantiate the score for this category.

(2) Environmental Benefits

	Points
If the purpose of the proposed system contributes to the environmental goals and objectives of other Federal, State, or local programs, **award 10 points.**	
Award points only if the applicant provides documentation from an appropriate authority supporting this claim.	10

Documentation in the file to substantiate the score for this category.
The DEPARTMENT has included a letter indicating that the project meets with goals and objectives of the agency with regard to environmental stewardship, sustainability and energy use reduction.

(3) Commercial Availability

	Points
If the proposed system or improvement is currently commercially available and replicable, **award 5 points.**	
If the proposed system or improvement is commercially available and replicable and is also provided with a 5 year or longer warranty providing the purchaser protection against system degradation or breakdown or component breakdown, **award 10 points.**	10

Documentation in the file to substantiate the score for this category.
The project is commercially available and professionally engineered as indicated by the manufacturer specification attached in Tab D, Project Summary. In Tab I, Technical Report, the dealer bid for the project is included and indicates acceptance of a five year warranty on the system.

(4) Technical Merit (To be completed by the agency or NREL)

	Points
Carry forward score from technical review sheet. Maximum score possible is 35 points.	35

(5) Readiness

If the applicant has written commitments, prior to the Agency receiving the complete application, from the source(s) confirming commitment of:

	Points
50% up to but not including 75% of the matching funds, **award 5 points.**	
75% up to but not including 100% of the matching funds, **award 10 points.**	
100% of the matching funds, **award 15 points.**	15

Documentation in the file to substantiate the score for this category.

FIGURE 10.1

(Continued)

The project has 100 percent of the financing needed to begin the project and complete the project in full. This financing is verified by a bank letter included from BANK.

(6) Small Agricultural Producer/Very Small Rural Business

If the applicant is an agricultural producer producing agricultural products with a gross market value of:

	Points
less than $600,000 in the preceding year, **award 5 points**.	
less than $200,000 in the preceding year, **OR** is a Very Small Rural Business as defined in 4280.103 (a business with less than 15 employees and less than $1 million in annual receipts), **award 10 points**.	

Documentation in the file to substantiate the score for this category.

The applicant has fewer than 15 employees and less than $1 million in annual receipts. Per 2010 tax returns, the applicant has a gross income of $_____.

(7) Simplified Applicaiton

	Points
If an applicant is eligible for and uses the simplified application process **or** if the project has total eligible project costs of $200,000 or less, **award 5 points**.	**5**

Documentation in the file to substantiate the score for this category.

The project has a total cost of $. which is less than the $200,000 total cost needed for a simplified application.

(8) Previous Grantees and Borrowers

	Points
If the applicant has not been awarded a grant or loan under this program within the 2 previous Federal fiscal years, **award 5 points**.	**5**

Documentation in the file to substantiate the score for this category.

The applicant has not received a 9006 or 9007 grant in the past. Certification to this is included in Tab D.

(9) Simplified Payback

A maximum of 15 points will be awarded for either renewable energy systems or energy efficiency improvements; points will not be awarded for more than one category.

(i) Renewable energy systems, including flexible fuel pumps - if the simple payback of the proposed project is:

	Points
Less than 10 years, **award 15 points**.	
10 years up to but not including 15 years, **award 10 points**.	
15 years up to and including 20 years, **award 5 points**.	**n/a**
Longer than 20 year, **award 0 points**.	

Documentation in the file to substantiate the score for this category (see 4/14/11 Interim Rule, 4280.103 Definitions, for complete Simple Payback criteria & calculations)

For **energy generation** projects, the calculation for simple payback is as follows =
Total Project Costs (including REAP Grant) of $ divided by (*Sum of ANI+Int+Depr $) =   **yrs simple payback**
*(Average Net Income (ANI) $ + Interest Expense $ + Depreciation Expense for the project $ = $)

For **energy replacement**, the calculation for simple payback is as follows =
Total Project Costs (including REAP Grant) of $ divided by Dollar Value of Energy Generated $) =   **yrs simple payback**

For **flexible fuel pumps**, the calculation for simple payback is as follows =
Total Project Costs (including REAP Grant) of $ divided by (*Sum of INI+Int+Depr $) =   **yrs simple payback**
*(Increase in Net Income (INI) $ + Interest Expense $ + Depreciation Expense for the project $ = $)

Or

FIGURE 10.1

(Continued)

(ii) Energy efficiency improvements - if the simple payback of the proposed project is:

If the proposed project will return the cost of investment in

	Points
Less than 4 years, **award 15 points.**	
4 years up to but not including 8 years, **award 10 points.**	
8 years up to 12 years, **award 5 points.**	
Longer than 12 years, **award 0 points.**	

Documentation in the file to substantiate the score for this category (see 4/14/11 Interim Rule, 4280.103 Definitions, for complete Simple Payback criteria & calculations)

For **energy efficiency improvement projects,** the calculation for simple payback is as follows = Total Project Costs (including REAP Grant) of $ divided by Dollar Value of Energy Saved $ =   **yrs simple payback**

The applicant has a short payback period of XX years according to the independent energy audit.

Note: EEI projects calculate savings based on similar size capacity. If capacity changes, savings pro-rated to similar size of existing equipment/facility.

See 4/14/11 Interim Rule, 4280.103 Definitions, for complete Simple Payback criteria & calculations.

(10) State Director and Administrator Priorities and Points

	Points
State Director, for its State allocation under this subpart, or the Administrator, for making awards from the National Office reserve may **award up 10 points.**	
Points may be awarded if the application is for an underrepresented technology or for flexible fuel pumps or if selecting the application would help achieve geographic diversity. In no case shall an application receive more than 10 points under this criterion.	

FIGURE 10.1

(Continued)

- If the NOFA doesn't include a self-evaluation score sheet, ask the GFO for the one they use to score applicants (they might give it to you!). Or, ask them if you may see a list or some other example of how the grant will be scored once it is received.

- Score your application *before you decide to apply* as part of the feasibility and eligibility evaluation process.

GRANT SUBMISSION

It was almost time to relax and celebrate. Just one click was all that was left to do after two months of work. Just push SEND.

And then the lights went out.

Kent and Jared were both aspiring young middle managers brought together by their superiors to complete a large federal grant application. Their task was to assemble a grant request of $1.8 million for a renewable energy project that the firm had previously put off initiating due to lack of complete funding. If the grant dollars came through, the match could be sufficiently obtained between the firm, the technology vendor, and an investor. It was turning out to be one of the biggest projects of both of their careers. It also had high expectations from the top.

Neither of them had grant writing experience and the firm budgeted a grant preparer to assist. Along with her, they labored over the application for 63 days; Kent had been keeping track, saying he wasn't going to shave his beard or drink a beer until this application was done. They knew they were agonizing over revisions and cutting the timeline really short. Finally, it was done. With a midnight deadline the day of, Jared's index finger hovered over the touchpad of his laptop. With around 20 minutes to spare, at 11:40 P. M., he hit SEND. And then the power went out.

Stunned silence followed as the two colleagues stared at the black hole where the computer had been. Now, it was only darkness. For a moment, nothing happened. Kent fumbled in his pocket, grabbed his phone, and tapped the screen for light. The entire place was dark. Finding their way to the hallway, they saw that even the parking lot security lights were off. "What the—!" Jared swore, and Kent, hand on his fluffy goatee, began to cry.

What happened? Apparently, someone hit a powerline nearby and the transformer to their building went out, killing the power. About 20 minutes later the backup generators went on. Scrambling, the two guys rebooted their computers. Unfortunately, the company's security measures kicked in and they were locked out. It didn't matter, they were past midnight anyway and the grant's management submission system was locked. No more submissions would be accepted.

Believe it or not, all was not lost. In finally reaching the agency late the following Monday, they learned their application had actually made it in time. Somehow, the SEND had occurred just before the outage and clicked through the system. They had met the deadline. Kent could return to his normal clean-shaven self.

As you can see, submission should be given as much seriousness as the entire process. You never get another chance to make a first impression. If your first impression with the GFO is an application submission past the deadline, don't expect much. In fact, you may not even so much as receive the courtesy of a rejection letter.

> The actual grant submission itself should be given as much seriousness as the entire process.

Here's a brief discussion about the two primary ways you submit a grant application: hard copy or digitally.

Hard Copy

Submitting your grant in hard copy is still quite common. If the GFO requires the paper route, you may even find yourself making up to eight sets of hard copies to send along with your submission. That's correct: They are allowing *you* to bear the expense of creating copies for each grant reviewer.

In this situation, I like to deliver in person. There is something so cathartic about dropping that grant off and driving away. I usually get myself a treat on the way home, maybe a coffee or a glass of wine, maybe lunch with a friend I've neglected for the deadline, but I do something. Handing off the grant is a nice feeling, second only to receiving an award letter. I like to use the opportunity to network with the GFO staff if possible and shoot the breeze about the number of submissions they've received, whether there are any unique projects, or any other interesting tidbits I can glean. Especially if you are working with a federal agency, whether at the state or area or national office, they don't always receive a lot of callers and enjoy the conversation, I've found.

There are a couple cautions for this. Do not leave your package with just any random person. Just because the receptionist promises to deliver it, that's not good enough. Unless that person has a tracking system at his desk and is officially logging in applications, move higher up the ladder. If you cannot personally see the grant program manager, ask for her supervisor or another person on the team. If you can't get anywhere with this, at a minimum, ask the receptionist or other gatekeeper to leave a voice mail while you're there, or preferably an e-mail, telling the official contact that a grant was delivered to him for such-and-such program and the exact time. Then, witness the person stamping the grant with a date stamp and get a copy to take home. Most of the time when I deliver the grants, someone from my office calls ahead to see if the program manager is there that day or if she has a system for accepting them/logging them in as received. I have almost always known the program manager, too, or have used the drop-by as a means to get better acquainted. Some grant writers will tell you not to bother GFOs on the grant intake deadline day, and for good reason. That's why I like to call ahead if I plan to hand deliver—I get the picture right away if they'd rather not see me.

Of course, you cannot always deliver in person. Mailing is quite the touchy situation, but many GFOs either accept mail or prefer it, despite those statements in the *Federal Register* about the "paperwork reduction act" (so much for that!). Be certain you pay for and obtain the best tracking information you can. Use a reputable carrier; I like to work with my local shipping store and become friends with the staff. I have brought them gifts before and I've chewed on some ears, too. This sounds harsh, but if you get the impression that the person weighing your package has been in the shipping business about three days, just leave and go to another store. I have had this happen—new person, wrong label or box or envelope or sticker or whatever (and who cares?), and my package is bound for a five-day journey when I paid for overnight. That is *not* acceptable.

Online Submission

Ways to submit digitally do differ and my preference for one over another is a bit like the story of the chicken and the egg. In one aspect I prefer the online system because I get an automatically generated tracking number and verification that I am on time. I have had to use this number to dispute with an agency that said they didn't receive my application by the deadline. On the other hand, if you work with a system with no tracking number and then the system locks you out (or some other atrocity occurs—it could be anything), by using e-mail submission directly to an individual, you (hopefully) have some luxury in that you can deal with a live human being on the other end of that e-mail, ideally, one who is sympathetic to you. Regardless of the route you take, be certain to cover your tracks with an e-mail verification from the agency, the automatic verification number generated when you submit, or even a screenshot of the submission acceptance screen. I really do prefer direct correspondence with someone telling me my application was received. I've used online submission systems where pushing SEND does nothing more than give me a popup with a message like "Your Application Has Been Submitted." That is *not* good enough for me. I want a better verification, so in that case I call and e-mail the agency, asking for an e-mail or at the *very least* a verbal confirmation that it was received. Most systems are better designed than that and will send out an automated e-mail, but you never know.

As you learned from the "Kent and Jared Submission Horror Story," your best option is to send in your application early. It can be hard to stay on deadline. I have submitted right at deadline online and hated it. Doing so the few times a client has pushed me there has most certainly taken years off my life for the stress (and you know it did for poor Jared!)

I will lie to my team about deadlines; I have no problem admitting this. They didn't pay me to be nice; they paid me to get them money, and the base minimum of that endeavor is *submitting on time*.

PERSPECTIVES ON PROSPERITY

> People acting in their own self-interest are the fuel for all the discovery, innovation, and prosperity that powers the world.
> —*John Stossel, columnist and political commentator*

In this chapter, I've shown how turning in your grant blind, that is, without any idea where you may score, is not necessary. The key concept from this part of the text is one of *knowing*. You can put some frame of reference around your grant's possible success and it can be done even if the grant agency doesn't provide a score sheet.

Applying for grants is in part a game of chance; you will not be the grant reviewer or the author of the award letter, and so you cannot guarantee success. However, improving your ability to win grants is very doable. Some of my suggestions in this chapter do perhaps seem self-serving, and my exuberance for obtaining confirmation of submission will seem haywire to some readers. However, most of these ideas are simply basic tips that work for me. In the same way your application is evaluated, you should also be both subjective and objective in how you package your grant for success. I know from experience that it takes both to win in a competitive industry.

CHAPTER ELEVEN

Surviving the Wait

It can be a nailing-biting, floor-pacing time, but now, you just have to wait. Here's what to expect.

"Hey, Sarah, Wes is on the line again—what should I tell him *this* time?" asked my office manager. Wes had called every week, on a Wednesday, following his grant submission six weeks ago.

"Same as before, I suppose, that it's only been six weeks and he'll know something before we will. Remind him that we don't expect to hear anything until fall. Thanks."

Over the next two months, I had correspondence with Wes often, though not because I had any new news for him. He continued to call, though we re-sent him the letter all applicants receive at submission, listing expectations (to the best of our knowledge) of when they will hear. One day, I arrived at my office at 8:45 A.M. to find Wes in the driveway. My office is a half-mile up the lane from my home, on the same rural property. Good thing I had done my hair.

"Wes! What a surprise," I said.

"I thought I would get better answers out of you if I just showed up at your place!" he snapped.

Wes was the one who was annoyed? I thought, but instead said: "Wes, I was about to make coffee, would you care for some?"

When my office manager arrived a few minutes later, she gave me a look that asked: "Should I call the police?" and I dismissed it with a smile. She pretended to get busy, but hovered around while I explained to Wes the same things we'd discussed over the last

60-some days, which were the same things we had spoken about before he applied. No, just because he had arrived at my office didn't mean I had different news for him. I was not the grant agency and I couldn't change the pace of their decision process. We were on target, I said, no worries at all. When I added that we just needed a little patience with the process, he wasn't convinced. This time, though, he wasn't annoyed, he was desperate.

"I just don't know if I can handle the pressure of waiting anymore!" Wes lamented as I showed him to his car an hour later. I noticed then that Wes wore a wedding ring.

"I wonder how his wife deals with this?" I thought.

HONING YOUR PATIENCE

Wes was not the first applicant who simply could not abide waiting for the grant status notification. I've worked with folks who have vacillated between Wes's near-neurosis and being nearly as excited to be done with the application process as they are when the good news arrives. Some clients want to take me out for a cocktail when we turn in an application; others make nice gestures toward me and my staff. We've received gift cards to a local ice cream shop and once even an invitation to spend the weekend fishing with the applicant's family. But regardless of their tolerance for waiting, all clients want to know: "What happens now?"

The grant-writing books I've read tend to fall short in the area of "what to expect when you're expecting." There may be work yet to do between submission and award, so you need to be ready. Once you receive an award there are definitely steps to take to ensure your funds are correctly dispersed. Cue Step 5 of the Prosperity Process: Patience. See Figure 11.1.

The fifth step in the process is no less important than the balance of the steps even though it is last and even though it occurs once the grant application is complete. Believe it or not, even though I told you in Chapter 10 that you couldn't control the approval process at this point, you can *still* screw up your application, your award process, or your payment process. That's why we need Step 5: Patience.

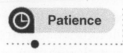

Wait for results
and work
collaboratively
with the grant
agency.

FIGURE 11.1

Patience

Source: Created by Brandrenew.

This chapter is your guide to the waiting game. Besides *yes* or *no*, there are other possible responses you could receive from the grant agency. I'm also going to work through the possible scenarios that can occur from now until the grant period is finished.

This chapter covers:

- The four possible responses you'll get from the GFO
- Approval to award process
- Corresponding with agency
- Grant agreement considerations
- Resubmission options
- Appeals
- Reporting and compliance

MY APPLICATION IS TURNED IN—NOW WHAT?

Though most aren't as stressed out about the waiting game as Wes, all applicants want to pester the GFO, or me, at least a little—it's hard not to wonder. It's like asking for someone's hand in marriage and being told "maybe," or "not yet." That may be extreme, but waiting on your grant application status is akin to applying to college and knowing it will be months before you get the answer. Your future plans may hang in the balance, so the wait can be torturous. Still, we have to stay patient; you can beg, you can plead, but you probably won't get the news any sooner if you do.

Knowing the duration of the review process in advance helps. Sometimes the NOFA will indicate the expected process time, and sometimes not. You might check with other applicants you know or, if you have a grant preparer, she may have experience with the program. Another option is to check the previously funded applications and track the process backward from the award announcement date to the previous year's open date. That is often a predictable indicator. Finally, call the GFO. Ask them for their best estimate or at least what happened in a previous year. Ask them how the correspondence will likely come to you. Will it arrive in an e-mail or in the mail? I've worked with several agencies that issue a press release with the winners before the notifications go out to those applicants who were denied. Talk about irritating—those *not* on the press release are waiting, assuming they are out of luck, but not certain. Don't write off the possibility of an award if this does happen to you. Until you have formal correspondence from the agency, assume nothing. In more than a handful of cases I've had applicants who *did* receive an award and yet were not listed on the publicity.

WHAT TO DO WHILE YOU WAIT

While some applicants must have grant money to begin their projects, some will be doing the work regardless of the grant award. In that case, clients ask me if they can start the work before receiving an answer. If you are considering this option, always *check with your grant professional or the GFO first*. This is extremely important, particularly with reimbursement grants. Handling expenses in the wrong order could jeopardize your grant funding.

> Handling expenses in the wrong order could jeopardize your grant funding.

There are two possibilities related to starting your project before grant award:

1. You may start the project as soon as the application is turned in without any problems. In this case, don't pay for any

expenses prior to the submission date and keep all of your documentation from that date forward.

2. You must wait to begin incurring expenses until notification of award or even until grant agreement. This means that any costs you incur prior to grant award or agreement will not be covered by the grant.

THE RESPONSES

Here are the four potential contacts you'll have with the GFO following application submission (also see Table 11.1 for the options you have in response, which we discuss in what follows):

- Yes
- No
- Question
- Not now

They Said Yes!

Excellent news—this is what you've been waiting for, a *yes* for your application. I cover all things grant agreement in the next section, but for now, you need to react to the award letter. You will likely receive

TABLE 11.1 Summary of Possible Agency Responses

Formal Response from Agency	Your Options
Yes	Sign acceptance letter, review grant agreement, sign grant agreement
No	Appeal, resubmit, do nothing, contact with questions, request feedback
Question	Respond promptly, get advice if needed, gather what is required, know when you'll hear back
Not now	Answer questions promptly, gather additional documentation, determine if you'll continue to wait, or pass

a hard-copy letter from the GFO notifying you of your award. If you did submit through an online system, you might receive an e-mail instead; however, many organizations still send paper for this notice. I've worked with a few GFOs that actually call the awardees, letting them know to expect an e-mail or letter. It is time to be excited, but don't just celebrate—you need to *react* to that letter fairly quickly.

First, respond to the grant award letter, formally accepting the grant. There will be a date on the letter by which you must respond. Don't ignore this. The GFO absolutely could offer your award to the next-lower-scoring application if you do not appear to have accepted it.

Next, you need to find out about the grant agreement and what is involved. Sometimes, the award letter will serve as an agreement and sometimes it will include an agreement in the package they send you. With online submissions and e-mail award notifications, I've seen the award e-mail accompanied by a link to download and sign the grant agreement. Seek out an agreement of some kind. Finally, it is possible that the GFO will prefer to meet you in person and sign the agreement at their office or yours.

For more information about grant agreement considerations, see the next section.

Oh, No, I Got Denied!

If your grant is denied, read the letter carefully and be certain to understand what happened. Look for the following clues as to what went wrong:

- Was it deemed ineligible?
- Was your score lower than what was needed for funding?
- Did the GFO offer feedback for denial?

I hope most GFOs offer some form of feedback to denied applicants, but I can tell you that they don't always. When it comes to feedback, I've seen canned denial letters with nothing useful to the applicant in them—it's irritating but it's possible. When that happens, applicants are frustrated, and rightfully so. If you do want feedback on your application (I certainly would), ask for it. Do this courteously. I would write or e-mail the agency, rather than call. This allows you to be concise. Also, if you are angry, hopefully you'll cool off while writing rather than bursting out with something rude on the phone. Your grant professional may also be able to request this feedback for you, although the agency could demand you personally give permission verbally or in writing to provide that information to a party other than you. Either way, *start by thanking the GFO*. Then, clearly ask your questions and request a score sheet or evaluation criteria. Finally, ask them to respond to you within a certain number of weeks (I know, that sounds like a long time, too). You may also request a phone call to discuss, if you think that would be helpful. The GFO may or may not offer you a score sheet, but I've found that most will if asked. If you are serious about wining grants and intend to apply again, how you handle this process is critical—especially if you ever want to work with this GFO. *Be completely professional at all times*. If handled correctly, this *no* could be temporary. If handled poorly, it could be permanent. Case in point: I've had three applicants over the course of my career that received a denial due to their score being lower than what was required to win the grant. However, in all cases, they eventually ended up with the money because one of the higher-scoring applicants ahead of them was unable to accept the funds and my applicant was offered the money. Stay positive.

What's a *Resubmit*? At this point, you may still have some options. If it is not mentioned in the letter, contact the GFO to learn if there is a resubmission process and if you qualify for that option. A resubmit can work in a variety of ways. You may be able to send your application back in during the next funding round without changing a thing. You may be able to make changes, based on the GFO's feedback, and submit again. In this case, you could receive a higher score and that may be the ticket to cash. What bothers most entrepreneurs about this process is, again, the wait time. Depending on the grant program, the resubmit-to-award process could be quite long or fairly brief. For example, I often use the American Honda Foundation's grant program.[1]

This program is open four times a year, so unfunded applications may be able to submit multiple times. The USDA REAP program, covered in Chapter 10, is open once a year, but allows resubmits in certain cases. The resubmit process is a long wait: Because awards are made only once a year, the applicant must wait for the next time the program opens and the next year's award date. It could be 18 months before an answer on the resubmit.

Should I Appeal? Besides accepting the *no* or attempting to resubmit, your other option is an appeal. Most denial notification letters will describe the right to appeal, if they offer a formal process. Government grants usually do.

Appeals are not my favorite idea because they are difficult to win. Of the thousands of grant applications I've submitted, I've done only two appeals. I won them both because I was 90 percent certain (darn sure!) I could help my client win an award. I've had many other cases where I was tempted to appeal and didn't believe we would win so I chose not to mount the effort. Here's why: Besides losing the grant, you should also be concerned about potential damage you might do to your relationship with the agency if you appeal. I'm not suggesting that you should not exercise your right when it's given; however, you should be certain you could win. Let's face it: The GFO staff is not going to enjoy their judgment being formally questioned; it makes them look bad.

Consider an appeal carefully and seek assistance with this decision. Usually, there is a window of time to appeal, so don't run at this process in fury. A low-scoring application is not solid grounds for appeal. Not all grant professionals will agree with this statement. Before I would consider an appeal of any kind, I need to understand the agency's reasoning behind the denial letter. Then, I move straight to the facts. Remember, grants are subjectively evaluated and your appeal will be subjectively reviewed to a certain

---

1. corporate.honda.com/america/philanthropy.aspx?id=ahf.

extent, too. So, if you want to appeal, use the NOFA and the grant regulations as your grounds. Let me give you an example.

A few years ago, I received calls from two applicants to the same program, just days apart. Both had been denied funding on the grounds of grant eligi-

---

A low-scoring application is not solid grounds for appeal.

---

bility. You know that I am serious about determining eligibility before an application. As you might expect, I was shocked with this result. I also noticed that the same area office of the GFO scored both applications. Pondering any connection, I realized that office had been experiencing high personnel turnover in the last year. I made a call and learned that, between the time we turned in applications and the time the notices were provided, the grant program manager had left. A new person, from another division of the agency, had taken his place. Calling the new individual, I learned his experience with the program was zero. In fact, he joked that I could probably educate him on the grant for as many of these as I'd completed.

So, I did appeal on the grounds that the inexperienced person misread the regulations on eligibility. A mediator was appointed. Acting on the applicant's behalf, we (the program manager for the grant, his supervisor at the GFO, the mediator, and I) had a few calls. I presented the regulation as evidence. The new person's supervisor quickly realized the error and we were able to reverse the denial decision for both applicants.

How Should I Answer That Question from the GFO? Number three on the list of possible correspondence post-submission is a question from the GFO. Typically, receipt of a question indicates a good situation, though many applicants get nervous about answering. A *question* is like getting a *maybe* or an *almost*. They may be calling to clarify, they may be calling to request updated documentation or request more recent material, such as the most recent year's financial projections or tax returns. Those are simple to handle, so go ahead. Or, maybe the GFO is looking for ways to split your application off from the herd and rule it out—but, surely *that* would never happen, right?

Well, it does, but not for any malicious reasons you may assume. You know by now that the GFO has only a certain pot of money to award. Once they've reviewed applications, there will be a bottom end of obvious noes and a top end of obvious yeses. Then there is the malleable middle. If your application falls in that group, it's question time. How you respond could move you either to File 13 or to an award letter. They may also use this time to decide how to split up the dwindling pot of money and offer you and other applicants a smaller award than you requested based on the conversation.

In discussing agency questions, some grant writers would start by saying, "Just be honest and just be yourself!" I'm not Pollyanna—we're talking about money here, so there is no room for joking. Before you respond, *think*.

Please do not interpret this discussion as any encouragement or endorsement to be dishonest. It is not. I am simply telling you that I have a strict "Do not accidentally screw up your grant by providing information you don't need to provide" policy. If you receive a call about something more interesting than basic documentation, ask the GFO to explain the context of the question. Ask them what they are trying to determine by looking into the issue. When I complete very technical grants for big construction projects, these challenging queries are the norm. I recommend the applicant contact me before discussing the project with the GFO and that we schedule a conference call so I can prepare. I want to have the application and documentation in front of me and be fully focused. I keep the regulations and the grant guidance document handy in case I need to refer to something during our call. For technical projects, I will need assistance from the engineer who designed the system or the project developer, so I make certain they are present. Usually, these calls go just fine—the GFO obtains what it needs to make a decision and we move on to an award letter.

We live in a time of great scrutiny around grant funding, whether from federal or corporate sources. I believe it is completely fair that we, the public, question the judgment of some of the grant awards that have been made. As such, GFOs are cautious these days.

The week that the Solyndra federal loan guarantee disaster broke in the news, I was scheduled for such a call with a federal agency reviewer and a client. The reviewer said to me: "I believe this application is quite sound, but in light of what is going on I need to make double-sure that if I award this and the Secretary gets a call from CNN about this program, he can stand behind the awardees fully."

Questions from the agency will happen, especially if you request a great deal of money. Expect them and handle them expeditiously but with care. A question will often lead to a *yes*, but I've had situations where our responses have led to a *no*. I encourage applicants to slow down and prepare before proceeding to answer. This is a perfect example of the importance of assembling a solid project team. Having experts on call will pay dividends.

GFO Correspondence Tips:
- Be honest, be thorough, and be brief.
- Seek assistance from the project team before responding.
- Understand the GFO's reasoning for the questions.
- Take time to assess your material and prepare.
- Consider scheduling a call with key people to prep.

Does *No* Mean *No*, Or *Not Now*?

The other side of the *no* coin is *not now*. This response is entirely possible, though it vexes some of my applicants as much as being denied. Don't be alarmed; relax and let the GFO explain the options to you so you come away from the conversation understanding when you will receive a final decision. Ask if there is anything you can provide to assist them in this decision. When you receive a *not now* response, it is usually due to the agency's inability to complete its program awards or because you are an alternate. Just hold on.

Possible Reasons for Not Now:
- Funding ran shorter than expected.
- You are an alternate.

- Program funding was discretionary.
- Government shutdown.
- Temporary hold or freeze on program funds.
- Administrative delays (no one is in the job role to dole out the funds).

One final possibility in the *maybe* category is that the GFO will offer you less than you requested. I have seen this occur with federal programs fairly often, so don't be surprised. Accepting less money than you requested is a strategic decision for you. Some applicants simply cannot take the award if it is less because they lack the funds available to cover the balance of the project. The GFO may ask you to prove that you could bring the matching funds now required; if not, they may not extend the lower award offer formally.

A couple of years ago, I was working with an entrepreneur who had developed a new technology and was readying it for commercialization. We applied for a $500,000 grant. The GFO offered him $75,000, take it or leave it. He chose to leave it. In his case, the red tape of dealing with a governmental entity was not worth it for $75,000. At $500,000, he was willing to do what it took, but for the number offered, it just didn't work. A few other programs I worked with ended up being converted from a grant to a loan program. The agency called the applicant and indicated he could receive a loan for the amount he had requested in grant funding. As you can see, the *not now* option presents several possibilities.

As you await the final verdict, keep faith and stay on top of your funding opportunity. You should contact the GFO at regular intervals, watch any announcements from the agency, and, most importantly, understand whether you can start the project at this point. If you cannot, determine the cost to your organization that this situation creates. For example, if you know that you must begin the project and you cannot continue to wait on grant funding, tell the GFO as early as possible that you won't accept the grant, even if you get an award at a later date.

THE GRANT AGREEMENT

Now that you've received an award, you're ready to sign the grant agreement. My advice is to read this document very carefully. You might want to seek legal counsel before signing this document. Examine any deadlines, due dates, and other timelines. You had to include some timelines in your grant proposal. Hopefully, you can still meet those without a problem. If there is an issue, discuss it with the GFO now. The need to shift a timeline doesn't necessarily negate your award. Be certain you are aware of any processes, contractor requirements, or reporting needs, which I cover in the next section. To ensure that you can meet the terms, this is a good time to check in with your expected contractors to discuss the expectations with them. It is possible that your contractors may be required to sign some documentation, too, which could include provisions about their wages, equal opportunity, or even the quality standards for equipment and products they will use on your project.

I Have This One Little Change . . .

Monday morning at 9 A.M., Julia, a program manager from a state agency, called me. She was frantic. I knew Julia fairly well; she'd been at the agency several years and I submitted a handful of successful applicants each year. Our working relationship was good, which was the reason for the courtesy of her call.

"I wanted to talk to you first before I called the applicant," she began. "This company is in jeopardy of losing their entire grant."

"What happened? The project looked great a couple days ago," I said, nausea spreading across my stomach like a wave. This project had been a tough one all along. We had struggled through the application with the applicant's back-and-forth last-minute changes. They had been a little difficult to please. The award was $525,000, sizeable for the agency in question. To make matters worse, they had been a referral from a very important customer of one of my very best clients. All the reasons I didn't want this going sideways flew around my mind.

"For starters, they've already hired contractors without the final approval we require and construction has started. Then, they e-mailed late yesterday to say that they weren't doing the boiler replacement and the energy-monitoring systems upgrade and wanted to make sure we'd still pay for the tanks and conveyor system even those won't be used with the renewable energy system anymore." She went on with more details, but I already knew the story: The awardee wanted the money but didn't want to do the project for which they'd applied. This could be a bad situation.

"Sarah, this project was a slam-dunk for the grant program, but if we can't get something figured out, I'll have to pull all the funding we committed," Julia said.

I'll spare you the details of the ensuing meetings, phone conferences, and haggling that resulted following this revelation. Though the awardee knew they were to complete the project as applied, they wanted to do something different now that they had the money and assumed that the agency wouldn't mind. In the end, the applicant got lucky. Although the agency did not give them grant funding for the portion of the project they completely changed, they did receive the balance of the funding for the portion they left as-was in their application. The GFO worked with the applicant. I was relieved. But, I have seen other situations where the agency simply pulled the funding entirely because the applicant's overall scope of the project changed and thus did not meet their original award criteria.

Plans do change, but the GFO has a limited capacity for understanding. It is not because the agency is trying to be difficult. The issue with project changes after award harks back to the question of whether your project still meets both the requirements they are seeking to fulfill and the mission they are charged with furthering. It can also be an issue of scoring. In a grant program where the project's years to return on investment is part of the scoring criteria, how does that payback change if you go from buying one kind of technology to another? If your desired change to the project potentially changes the score (meaning, it now scores lower), the GFO is going to have a problem.

Here is the bottom line: Do not apply for a grant with the intention that you will do something other than what is in your application. If a change is imminent, however, discuss the problem with the GFO candidly and ask them to work with you on a solution. It is possible that you can work that out and retain your grant award.

OTHER QUESTIONS TO ASK

While you are corresponding about the agreement, ask about any other commitments they may have for you going forward. Be advised, you may be asked to participate in publicity for the GFO. Ask them about this prospect and the type of promotion they do for their awardees. I've found that the more local the GFO, the more personalized the promotion. This can be a wonderful opportunity for the applicant who appreciates it. Or, it may not fit for you strategically. Ask them about their intentions. Many GFOs are sensitive to possible applicant concerns around publicity, but they do have some requirements on which they won't bend. For example, you may not be able to keep them from listing your name and the award amount on their website or in a press release. They may also be charged with providing a list of awardees to any member of the public requesting the information. This probably has nothing to do with promotion and is more than likely a requirement of their governing body to make public information about how their money is spent.

My company also does publicity for our applicants, but we ask if it is acceptable before doing an article. If you view my website, you'll find videos, testimonials, and a few news releases with awards. There are a few client logos, too. Many of our projects go untoasted in the public, however, because the entrepreneurs I work with do not want the added publicity until they are ready to handle it. If you are partnered with another organization, be sure you agree on the publicity each will do if awarded.

Other types of public award notification may be negotiable, however. For instance, I work with a state agency that honors awardees at the state capitol. The governor speaks, hands out the award plaques, and has photo opportunities with each applicant. Here's another scenario: In 2010, the USDA Office of the Secretary of Agriculture contacted one of my successful applicants and asked if they could do a roadshow stop at his farm. A few days later, multiple staffers and a representative for the Secretary descended on the guy's place and media followed. They interviewed the farmer about his project, toured his site, and read a list of names of all the other awardees in that state. His project was certainly promoted.

TRANSITIONING FROM APPLICANT TO AWARDEE

Congratulations! You have a new title. You are no longer "Applicant." You are now "Awardee." Your objective is accomplished.

When Do I Get Paid?

If you haven't wondered already, the receipt of an award letter will certainly prompt you to get excited about receiving your hard-won cash. There are a couple of possibilities. They vary widely, based on the GFO's sophistication and systems. A few grant types, most likely those for programing and sometimes those for research, will pay you up front, before the work has begun. Usually, they will pay for a portion of the work and you'll be asked to submit satisfactory reports to receive additional installments. When I work with construction grants, they are universally reimbursement based. So, the awardee pays for (at minimum) the portion of the work covered by grant, submits receipts, potentially meets (in person or over the phone) with the GFO, and is reimbursed. It is also possible that you pay for and complete your project in its entirety before you receive any cash. Again, learn about these payment timelines during your grant agreement evaluation.

As finally receiving your grant dollars is the goal, you should strive to remain organized and ready for a seamless process. All should go well from this point on; however, sometimes there are unforeseen glitches. Some of these are beyond your control, like a contractor suddenly going out of business, or a government shutdown. In those cases, you must simply keep calm and carry on. Still other glitches are the awardee's fault—these are preventable, so read on.

There are two major details to manage: *project process* and *vendor payee documentation*. Your GFO really wants to send the money your way at this point. However, if you can't provide the documentation the agency requires, you won't receive your funds; that was just illustrated in my story about the project change. We cover reporting in the next section, but prepare for the inevitable reporting process by organizing at the outset with a project management plan. You know that I advocate using a project manager. What will the project manager do following grant agreement? Here are some possibilities:

- Act as the main point of contact for the GFO.
- Build a list of GFO responses required, what is involved in each, who is needed to sign off on the reports, and when all are due based on reporting requirements.
- Maintain a list of expenses, contractors, vendors, project partners, and the contact information for each.
- Manage the anticipated project timeline with actual project completion status.
- Make payments or handle funds dispersal.
- Complete any formal reports.
- Generally manage compliance with all regulations, including possible wage requirements.
- Keep a file of project successes, publicity, and other accolades to share with the agency.

Finalizing the Grant Period and Closing Out

In many instances, the project management role will be fairly simple, perhaps including one annual report and a final report at the conclusion of the grant period. However, other grant programs are extremely laborious during the grant period and require more regular attention, including possible quarterly reports, statistics of how the project has progressed, and frequent site inspections.

Common areas of compliance include labor and prevailing wage laws. Compliance may be required by the awardee or by contractors

---

GRANTS GURU GLOSSARY

Davis Bacon Act compliance: The Davis Bacon Act applies to all contractors or subcontractors that are working on a federally funded contract that exceeds the amount of $2,000 for the construction, alteration, or repair of a public building. Under the Davis Bacon Act, contractors must pay their currently employed laborers no less than the locally prevailing wage and fringe benefits. The Department of Labor determines the local prevailing wage rates. The prevailing wage provisions for the Davis Bacon Act apply to the "Related Acts" where federal agencies assist projects through grants, loans, loan guarantees, as well as insurance.
Source: http://www.dol.gov/whd/govcontracts/dbra.htm.

---

being used to complete the work needed to begin the awardee's project. One such labor law is the Davis Bacon Act.

Reporting

If your grant was paid via reimbursement, you're already doing some reporting. However, for grants extending into six months or more and requiring multiple years to complete, regular reporting is to be expected. Some agencies will give you actual schedules and hold up payouts if you are late, so, put those dates on your calendar! Some agencies have specific forms; others just require a set of information written in your own words. In addition to what your specific GFO requires, at a minimum keep the following on hand for reporting:

- Grant agreement date
- Grant period closing date
- Dates ordered equipment/supplies
- Contracted vendors
- Dates equipment arrived

Major Equipment Piece	Cost	Down Payment Amount	Date Down Payment Paid	Balance Due Q1	Balance Due Q2	Balance Due Q3	Balance Due Q4	Have Receipt/Invoice (Y/N)

FIGURE 11.2

Contractor Expenses Template

- Contractor start dates
- Contractor end dates

The easiest way to track this is to create a separate spreadsheet by contractor for each expense. Figure 11.2 shows a sample I've used.

The agency may require you to update your information with them each year or you may have to add an additional annual report. That should be spelled out in the agreement.

Closing Out the Grant and Project Periods

In addition to regular project period reporting, some GFOs have a formal grant closeout process. This will certainly include a set of final reports where the awardee certifies that the funds have been dispersed and the project is complete. There are a number of federal programs requiring awardees to present a formal poster or talk about their project and accept Q&As from a live panel. You may have to pay for the trip out-of-pocket. For construction projects, your GFO may require documentation that your local government officials and environmental regulators are satisfied with the project's completion. The GFO may even request feedback from you on the grant program. While usually optional, I encourage awardees to comment—candidly, specifically, and courteously. Finally, should you plan to participate in more grant funding, evaluate the process for yourself. Examine your role and those of team members and partners, and evaluate how the experience was positive and identify aspects for improvement.

PERSPECTIVES ON PROSPERITY

Much effort, much prosperity.

—Euripides

You've done the work. You've put in the time. You've certainly used a mountain of effort. Your payday is on its way, right? I hope so, but I can't say for certain whether you'll win your first grant or the twenty-first grant. I do know that if you hadn't tried there would be no opportunity to find out.

This chapter has covered the final step in my Five-Step Prosperity Process: Patience. Being an entrepreneur myself made selecting *patience* for an actual step in my grant funding process quite logical. Once we have completed one task, especially one that has required focus and great effort, we entrepreneurs are ready for results. And, we're ready to move on. Going back-and-forth with the GFO can tax our patience and is against our nature.

Here again are the key aspects of my patience step as highlighted in the previous chapter. Once your application is submitted, the following may occur:

- You may (or may not) receive a confirmation that your application is being reviewed.
- You may receive questions from the GFO.
- You may get a *yes* right away.
- You may get a *no*.
- You may get a *maybe* or one of the other options, including accepting less than you requested.

No matter what, you'll have to wait at least a short while for a *yes* or *no*.

Occasionally, we get grant results quite quickly, but most of the time, grant funding is not immediate. Good things can come to those who wait. Prosperity follows work, and the work ethic is another trait successful entrepreneurs embody.

CONCLUSION

Grant Writing Secrets

You might be thinking, "What if I'm looking for a few ways to grease the skids? Do you have any special ideas or insider secrets to winning a grant?" Yes, I've got a few for you.

In my Five-Step Prosperity Process (Project, Peruse, Ponder, Prepare, and Patience), I've shared with you the model I use to decide what grants to seek, when to use them, and how to apply for them. You've learned that there are dollars out there worth seeking, where to find them, how to determine your likelihood of winning them, and how to strategically evaluate the grant market-place for your business. We've looked at application pieces and we've discussed the "what to expect when you're expecting" process post-application. Now, I'm ready to wish you well in the pursuit of grant funding.

Before we say goodbye, I want to offer you a few more tips. Let's call them *my personal-best secrets*. I hope these will help you in your grant funding search.

Ten Things to Do Every Time for Grant Success:
1. Know where you stand. *Score* your grant application before you decide to apply.

2. Meet your funders. Don't go into the process blind. Make connections that matter; have conversations that yield useful information. It pays to get to know those people who are evaluating your applications.

3. Never focus on yourself. Highlight the GFO's missions and explain how many people will gain from your project. The GFO knows you'll benefit from the dollars—tell them why *they will*.

4. *Never* apply unless you're positive that you're eligible.

5. Appoint a project manager—you don't need an outside consultant necessarily, but you do need someone who cares enough to own this project from NOFA to submittal, from first glance to grant closeout. Find someone assertive and dedicated. Try to avoid deadline duds who hold your project hostage near the end.

6. Find your zone—where creativity and intuition meet critical analysis and laser-point attention to detail.

7. As the project owner, be all in. Don't just turn your application over to a grant preparer and hope for the best. Learn the industry and direct the process.

8. In the world of grant funding, payment follows project. Work diligently on the front end of the application process to ensure your project is a solid fit for the grant program. Identify the categories your GFOs fund, then build a project using your ideas and needs around that.

9. Make your own *90 percent rule* for evaluating your tolerance for risk, your feasibility of grant success, and the strategic implications that winning a grant award brings to your business.

10. Build your own process. Take my five steps, modify them, and figure out the replicable, workable system that yields green for you!

PERSPECTIVES ON PROSPERITY

> Prosperity suits some people, and they blossom best in a glow of sunshine; others need the shade, and are the sweeter for a touch of frost.
> ——*Louisa May Alcott*, Jo's Boys

I wondered how best to use this quote, taken from the novel *Jo's Boys*, which is the sequel to *Little Men*, because while I liked the tone of it, the comparison between "the glow of sunshine and the touch of frost" seemed dissonant. These two things are opposites and seem out of sync. But that is the very point of this book: a grant funding book about *not* applying for grants—or better, intelligently considering *whether* to apply for grants based on your actual needs.

I want you to take away from reading this book a clear point of view about whether you think grant funding is an excellent fit for your company or will not work under any circumstances. If you make either decision based on reading my work and are better for it, I've succeeded and this book's intent has shown its merit:

- Grant funding is possible for entrepreneurs.
- Grant funding is available to entrepreneurs.
- Grant funding may assist entrepreneurs.
- But, grant funding is not for everyone.

There is much to be said for those who will never accept a dime of another's money—though, we all get help somewhere, be it a lucky break or a financial windfall; we're never solely responsible for our success. Grants are like the dissonance in the Alcott quote— at once so helpful and yet so frustrating. They can make great sense to one person and be complete nonsense to another. That's okay— you're an entrepreneur and you're used to making decisions based on what you know you can do and not what the world says is possible. After reading this book you can now decide with surety whether grant funding is a good fit for you.

It does not matter whether you stay in the shade or find the sun: The direction of your business is yours alone to decide. This book presents to you just another option in that long journey of entrepreneurship. Whether you take this route on your path to prosperity is up to you.

Sarah Aubrey

APPENDIX A

Project Evaluation Tool

This evaluation tool uses a combination of simple questions about your project and a chart where you can list whether you have items generally needed for a grant application. Working through this will help to determine how ready you are to create a project that can be used in a grant application. Please answer all questions thoroughly and honestly.

- **By the end of this assessment tool, before moving onto a grant application, you should be able to complete the following paragraph:**

    This is a project about _____ that involves _____ and is essential to you, the GFO, because _____ and impacts _____ (list people, change, or improvement), which I can measure by the following _____ (number) or measurements _____ (describe measurements). It will be completed by _____ (project team) with credentials such as _____. We will complete the project at a cost of _____. It will start on _____ (date) and finish on _____ (date).

- Complete the following checklist of items potentially needed to move your project forward:

Readiness Inquiry	Complete	In Progress	Resources Needed	Not Started	Not Applicable (N/A)
Business Documentation:					
Feasibility study					
Business plan					
Pro formas					
Tax returns					
Market surveys					
Intellectual Property:					
Patents					
Copyrights					
R&D studies					
Related studies or works					
Project Costs: What is the status of the following?					
Project cost					
Detailed budget					
Quote(s)					
Vendors					
Licenses/ certifications obtained					
Agreements					
Permits					
Timelines: What is the status of the following?					
Project start date					
Project end date					

Matching Funds:					
Cash on hand					
Investors					
Lenders					
In-kind contributions					
Entity Documentation:					
Articles of Incorporation					
EIN/TIN					
DUNS					
CAGE					

- **To score your readiness to move to the grant application process, complete the following short-answer questions. Assign one point to each question you can fully answer and no points to any questions you cannot fully answer:**

    1. Do you have a formal organizational structure? If so, what is it (LLC, S-Corp, 501(c)3, etc.)?

        _____

    2. Do you have a site or place of performance for the project? If so, do you have documentation of ownership or lease agreement?

        _____

    3. Do you know what outside resources, vendors, and services you need to make this project work?

        ☐ Yes   ☐ No   ☐ Unsure

    4. Have you done the research required to begin a project? If so, can you show documentation of your work?

        ☐ Yes   ☐ No   ☐ Unsure

        If yes, please explain documentation below:

        _____

5. Do you have at least 3-5 priority activities that you can clearly describe? If yes, list them below:

   ☐ Yes ☐ No ☐ Unsure

   (1) _____

   (2) _____

   (3) _____

   (4) _____

   (5) _____

6. Do you have 3–5 benefits for you/your community? If so, please list:

   (1) _____

   (2) _____

   (3) _____

   (4) _____

   (5) _____

7. Can you describe in 2 sentences or less what the need is that your project will address and how? If so, do so here:

   _____

   _____

8. Can you clearly describe your end customer or the targeted recipient of your project work? If so, do so in 2-3 sentences below.

   _____

   _____

9. Do you have documented additional funding sources beyond grant funding? If yes, list them below:

   ☐ Yes ☐ No ☐ Unsure

   (1) _____

   (2) _____

   (3) _____

   (4) _____

10.   Do you know the exact project cost?

☐ Yes   ☐ No   ☐ Unsure

- **Please determine your project's readiness for grant funding based on the following score:**

Answered 0–5   Not ready for grant funding; put together more project information

Answered 6–8   Possibly ready for a funding search, but not a grant application

Answered 9 or 10   Ready to move forward with the next step in a grant application

APPENDIX B

Grant Planning Tool

This readiness assessment uses simple questions that will help to determine whether you or your team are prepared to successfully begin a grant application. Please answer all questions thoroughly and honestly.

- **By the end of this assessment tool, before moving onto a grant application, you should be able to complete the following paragraph:**

    This is a project about _____ that involves _____ and is essential to you, the GFO, because _____ and impacts _____ (list people, change, or improvement), which I can measure by the following _____ (number) or measurements _____ (describe measurements). It will be completed by _____ (project team) with credentials such as _____. We will complete the project at a cost of _____. It will start on _____ (date) and finish on _____ (date).

- **Complete the following short-answer questions to the best of your ability:**

    Have you taken the project evaluation tool?

    ☐ Yes   ☐ No   ☐ Unsure

    Did you score at 9 points or above?

    ☐ Yes   ☐ No   ☐ Unsure

Have you successfully applied for grants in the past?

☐ Yes   ☐ No   ☐ Unsure

Do you have a specific grant for which you'd like to apply? If so, please list the name of the program.

_____

Have you researched grant funding opportunities? If so, please list them.

_____
_____

Grant Readiness Assessment:

Are you ready for this process now?

☐ Yes   ☐ No   ☐ Unsure

Have you done the research required at this point? If so, can you show documentation of your work?

☐ Yes   ☐ No   ☐ Unsure

If yes, please explain below:

_____
_____

Are you willing to have your project publicized at this point?

☐ Yes   ☐ No   ☐ Unsure

Are there any PR and local acceptance issues?

☐ Yes   ☐ No   ☐ Unsure

Is your project controversial?

☐ Yes   ☐ No   ☐ Unsure

Are there any barriers to getting started?

☐ Yes   ☐ No   ☐ Unsure

Do you have a project team? If yes, describe roles team members play:

_____

_____

Who in your area industry can support the project formally?

_____

Does your organization have access to funding beyond the grant request to complete the project (ie: possible required matching funds?)

☐ Yes   ☐ No   ☐ Unsure

Does your organization have a system in place to manage grant funding, vendor payouts, and grant reporting?

☐ Yes   ☐ No   ☐ Unsure

Have you evaluated the effects grant funding will have on your organization in the marketplace?

☐ Yes   ☐ No   ☐ Unsure

Do you have a clear mission statement and staff on board to execute it?

☐ Yes   ☐ No   ☐ Unsure

Do you have potential grant application or project partners identified?

☐ Yes   ☐ No   ☐ Unsure

Index